AF860011

For Kathy

&

To all those who have had to –
or may have to –
endure the ordeal of litigation.

LEGALLY BLIND

A Primer to Litigation

By

Mark L. Stockton

INFINITY
PUBLISHING.COM

Copyright © 2008 by Mark L. Stockton

All rights reserved. No part of this book shall be reproduced or transmitted in any form or by any means, electronic, mechanical, magnetic, photographic including photocopying, recording or by any information storage and retrieval system, without prior written permission of the publisher. No patent liability is assumed with respect to the use of the information contained herein. Although every precaution has been taken in the preparation of this book, the publisher and author assume no responsibility for errors or omissions. Neither is any liability assumed for damages resulting from the use of the information contained herein.

ISBN 978-0-7414-5621-2

Library of Congress Catalog Registration
Number: TXu 1-597-311

Published by:

INFINITY
PUBLISHING.COM

1094 New DeHaven Street, Suite 100
West Conshohocken, PA 19428-2713
Info@buybooksontheweb.com
www.buybooksontheweb.com
Toll-free (877) BUY BOOK
Local Phone (610) 941-9999
Fax (610) 941-9959

Printed in the United States of America

Published February 2013

ACKNOWLEDGMENTS

Any piece of work like this one is the product of many contributions. In this case, much that was contributed came from individuals who were not aware they were aiding any endeavor other than their own legal challenges. This group includes every attorney, every witness, every judge, and every other participant in any case in which I have been involved. Knowingly or unknowingly, the good guys and the bad guys all contributed something to a body of knowledge that has become the basis for this book. I thank them all – sort of.

In addition, there are a few other individuals who have contributed much. My wife, Kathy, not only shared the experience of several of the legal cases cited herein, but then had to relive each one during the two year period that I dug back through the documents and the memories that serve as reminders of challenges past. She was always supportive.

Jeffrey Olup, who wrote the Foreword to this book, served not only as fine legal counsel on more than one occasion, but also provided a legal perspective and a legal check for this text. His help, and his friendship, have always been appreciated.

Finally, I owe much to Joyce Davidson, who proof read this text (more than once), corrected my misspellings and my grammatical errors, and who simply added "flow" to the text. If you find this easy to read and easy to understand, you too owe Joyce a thank you.

I, of course, thank each of you who read this book, as well. I hope you find advice herein for which you will be thankful.

Mark L. Stockton

Contents

FOREWORD

Litigation. It is extraordinarily expensive, time-consuming, and emotionally, and, at times, physically draining. The outcome of any case is fraught with uncertainty. I can vaguely recall another author's admonition that litigation should be avoided like the plague. The very mention of the term conjures images of shark-like lawyers circling and preparing to strike.

I know. I swim with those fish.

There are those occasions, however, when an individual, business or other organization may be faced with the inexorable task of filing or defending a lawsuit. Many is the time that I have heard a client's lament who "never thought that they would ever have to be involved" in the litigation/trial process.

Even those experienced in the process will occasionally find themselves perplexed, or even outraged by a judge's decision or jury's verdict. As an aside, the notion that two individuals who may not even be able to agree on that evening's dinner selection gives one pause to consider how a jury of twelve could reach a verdict after a vigorously contested trial.

Over a decade ago, after substantial preparation and a hotly contested two-week jury trial (which I felt certain to win) my clients suffered utter defeat. To this day, I cannot fathom how that panel of jurors came to its decision. I could not explain the outcome to the clients, nor to anyone else, for that matter.

Much like the rest of life, there was no primer or textbook to which I could turn for guidance or answers or, for that matter, solace.

Years later, I was asked to meet with Mark Stockton who had then traveled cross country to Pennsylvania to discuss a number of legal issues and claims that he wished to pursue. It turned out that Mr. Stockton was also similarly faced with the unavoidable task of filing a lawsuit, or two.

I am flattered that he saw something enough in this writer so to entrust his (substantial) legal matters with me. For that, I remain grateful.

The journeys we shared and outcome(s) of those matters, as well as other significant legal battles in Mark's life, are for Mark to tell. More to the point, Mark's legal experiences have borne unexpected fruit: a primer on how to survive the litigation process – a valuable resource to the uninitiated and acquainted, alike.

I will insist on it as required reading for those clients engaged in the legal processes.

Dear reader must avoid the temptation to skip ahead to Mark's "My Advice to You" section without savoring and appreciating his real-world experiences in the text. One cannot enjoy the sizzle without the steak.

After twenty-some-odd years of litigation, trial and appeals court practice, I can, without hesitation or equivocation, state that Mark Stockton, and his wife, Kathleen Stockton, were folks for whom working was truly and completely enjoyable. I am privileged to put pen to paper in this Foreword.

Legally Blind is the end result of a wellspring of Mark's talents and experiences – the latter earned the hard way.

May his travails assist you in your trials.

Jeffrey T. Olup

INTRODUCTION

As our population continues to grow, so grows our national appetite for litigation. Our citizens are living longer and working longer, and with every passing year it becomes more likely that we'll be confronted by the need to defend ourselves against claims of impropriety or the need to go to court to claim or reclaim what is rightfully ours. This is true for everyone, regardless of age or employment status.

I am not a pessimistic person, but there is an adage that I have unfortunately found to be quite true. It goes like this:

"Whenever you acquire anything of value, there will always be someone who will try to take it away from you."

That someone might be the firm that manages your investments, the company you hired to build that addition on your house, the petty thief, or the neighbor next door. It is not altogether unlikely that you will someday find yourself in a position of having to go to court to recover something that has been unjustly taken from you, or to defend yourself against an allegation of wrongdoing. If and when that happens, you need to be prepared to deal with the process. If you're like most of us in America, you have a blind spot when it comes to our legal system.

According to a U.S. State Department publication dated August of 2004, "The federal and state court systems of the United States hear an estimated 100 million cases a year before approximately 2,200 federal justices and 31,000 state and local judges." The cost to the American public is impossible to quantify accurately, but the Tillinghast insurance consulting practice of Towers Perrin (a global professional-services firm) estimates the direct cost of tort (non-contract) litigation in 2006 was $261 billion. As the Pacific Research Institute points out, direct costs pale in the face of the indirect costs associated with tort litigation in our nation, which they estimate to be no less than $865 billion annually. Indirect costs were defined as "costs for such things as lost jobs and retirement savings, unnecessary deaths due to health care inaccessibility, lower investments in research and development, and a considerably lesser degree of economic competitiveness." No matter how you slice it, that's a lot of money. Litigation in America is big business.

The process of litigation is really quite unlike people's perception of "going to court" – if indeed they have any perception of it at all. Most of us have watched courtroom scenes in movies or on television; many of us have known someone who has been involved in a lawsuit, or have had some experience that leads us to believe we have a basic understanding of the process. Believe me, once you become involved in litigation on a personal level you will find it surprisingly more complex than you imagined, and you will wish you were better prepared. I speak from experience: I have been involved in several lawsuits in my 60 plus years, and I still wish I were better prepared.

I am not a lawyer. I am an independent businessman. I have been called an entrepreneur, and while I suppose I fit the classic definition, I prefer to think of myself as an independent businessman. During my years in business I have been sued once and I have brought suit against another on two related occasions. I have also been involved in a lawsuit as one of several parties joined in a real property title and access dispute. Being self-employed and having a somewhat flexible work schedule, I have been able to immerse myself in these cases to a degree others might find difficult. Consequently, I have learned a great deal from my direct involvement. This book draws on my first hand experience to provide you, the reader, with some information that I hope will prove quite useful should you become involved in a court case. It is my sincere hope that it will help you make better decisions that will result in a happier outcome. By that I don't imply that what I offer here will help you win your case. It might. In all probability it might prevent you from losing your case because you were totally unprepared, and it might help you cope better. Perhaps you won't be as apt to become disoriented by the process.

Although I know others who have had interesting and educational experiences at court, I have confined my references to cases that I have been involved in personally. While I have no reason to question the stories of others, I know the facts in the cases I have participated in, and I have the factual documentation to use as reference materials.

I confess that my batting average at court is poor; it's a solid .250 – hardly sufficient to qualify for the silver slugger award. Because most of my experiences at court have not been positive, most of the instances I relate deal with hazards to be avoided in the legal process. The examples therefore focus on the negative, because it is often from negative experience that we learn to find positive solutions. Besides, I'll bet that those with far better batting averages would not represent their courtroom experiences as altogether "positive."

This text is therefore intended to be instructional without being tedious, rather than purely entertaining. Above all, I hope you find it enlightening.

MY COURTROOM EXPERIENCES

As mentioned, I have been involved in several lawsuits. All have been litigated in State Courts. I don't intend to present all the details of each case, but I do want to provide a thumbnail sketch of each proceeding. These cases will serve as reference material for specific examples given later on in this book. I will point out that three of the four cases arose from business transactions I was involved in. It's reasonable to anticipate that the exposure to litigation might be higher for those actively engaged in commercial dealings. I became involved in the fourth, however, simply by virtue of the fact that my wife and I purchased a piece of land and built a home on it—something very commonplace in today's world.

<u>Sowerwine vs. Stockton (1982)</u>

This case involved a 1510 acre parcel of property located in Park County, Wyoming that I purchased from Mr. E.O. Sowerwine, Jr. and the Broken H Ranch Trust in June of 1981. Mr. Sowerwine's property was being foreclosed by his bank due to non-payment of the mortgage. He tried to refinance the mortgage, he tried to find someone who might partner with him in the ownership of the property, and he tried to find individual investors who might be willing to pay down the mortgage and help him develop a small part of the property – all without success. As a last resort, Mr. Sowerwine asked me if I would purchase a portion of his ranch (1510 acres out of a total of approximately 3,000 acres) for enough money to pay off all of his creditors—who were unimaginably numerous. He wanted a one-year option in which to repurchase 1505 acres of the property for a price that would insure me a profit on my investment, leaving me with a five acre parcel to compensate me for my trouble. My sole responsibility would be to put up the money; it was up to Sowerwine to find the capital to buy back the property and deliver it, in certified funds, to the Stockgrowers State Bank in Worland, Wyoming no later than June 22, 1982. If he succeeded, I had to provide him a deed to 1505 acres and notify him of my reimbursable expenses within five days. If he failed, the option would expire and nothing was required of me.

Although Sowerwine's asking price for the 1505 acres was substantial by the standards of the time (several hundred thousand dollars), I thought I might be able to borrow enough money to make the purchase. It appeared I would have no risk; either Sowerwine would repurchase the property, guaranteeing me five acres and a fixed profit after all my expenses, or I would retain the property. If Sowerwine was unable to make the repurchase, I thought I could sell a portion of the property to reduce the debt and lease out the remaining agricultural ground. The lower end of the property had a well with a pivot irrigation system and some good grazing land for livestock. All in all, it looked to me like a good investment.

I purchased the property according to the terms that Sowerwine had prescribed. The year came and went, and Mr. Sowerwine had made no earnest attempts to raise the repurchase money. In April, less than 90 days before the option was to expire, Mr. Sowerwine assigned his rights under the Agreement and Option to Repurchase to his son, E.O. Sowerwine III, with the hope that he, with his better credit standing, might be able to raise the necessary funds.

On June 10th, less than two weeks before the option was to expire, I received a call from my attorney saying that E.O. III had contacted him and was going to be able to repurchase the property. However, he had asked us to meet with him to discuss a modification to the terms of the original agreement. At that meeting, held June 12th and recorded with the consent of all present (that's how much I trusted the Sowerwines), he asked for an extension of time to get his money together. He also asked me to select and survey the five acre parcel I wished to retain so that he could have the exact legal description to the remaining 1505 acres in order to perfect his new mortgage. According to Sowerwine, the Federal Land Bank had agreed to loan him enough money to repurchase the property, but they wouldn't deposit the money with the Stockgrowers State Bank as the agreement prescribed, without first having the complete legal description of the land, less the five acres I intended to retain.

As an ex-banker I knew the legal description wasn't needed in order for Sowerwine to arrange his financing. The terms of the option required that he deposit the money with the Stockgrowers State Bank on or before June 22nd, and I was to have five days in which to deliver the deed to the bank and collect the money. If I didn't deliver the deed, I didn't get the money; it would never be at risk. I told Sowerwine that if the Federal Land Bank had truly agreed to make the loan, they would have no problem delivering the money to the bank pending delivery of the deed – transactions like that were not uncommon. (This is, in fact, precisely what the Federal Land Bank eventually did in 1983.)

My attorney and I both told Sowerwine I would not change the terms of our agreement without some sort of additional consideration. I told him that I was under no obligation to provide more time or to provide a legal description on the basis of an unsupported statement that he had located the repurchase money. I also reminded him that it was his obligation to tender the money as per the terms of the agreement, and had he and his father been more diligent and timely in their search, perhaps they could have raised the necessary funds within the agreed upon time period. Sowerwine would not consider discussing any additional consideration in return for my willingness to modify the original agreement, so I refused his requests. My attorney added that the assignment of the option from father to son was invalid since the Broken H Ranch Trust, a party to the option, was not a party to the assignment. He suggested that E.O. Sowerwine III obtain a new assignment from both his father (who was *not* a trustee of the Trust) and the person authorized to execute the document on behalf of the Trust.

After the meeting ended, my attorney and I tried to understand what had just occurred. The whole thing sounded fishy to us, and I told my counsel that I felt like I was being set up for a lawsuit.

The option to repurchase expired on June 22nd with no further contact from any of the Sowerwines. The repurchase money was never tendered.

I wasn't surprised (mad maybe, but not surprised) when E.O. Sowerwine III filed suit against me on September 21, 1982. In the Complaint, Sowerwine claimed I had used my influence as an ex-banker in the State of Wyoming to bar him from obtaining the financing necessary to make the repurchase. He also claimed that I had deliberately prevented him from exercising the option by failing to acknowledge the validity of the assignment of the option from his father to him, by refusing to have the property surveyed in order that I might give him a legal description before the option monies had been tendered (as required by the option agreement), and by refusing to grant him an extension of time in which to make good on the option. Bottom line: Sowerwine claimed that I had breached the implied Covenant of Good Faith and Fair Dealing that is contained in all contracts, and he should be given another opportunity to repurchase the land or be granted damages of $1,000,000.

In my response as Defendant in the suit, I stated that I had no responsibility to grant any of Sowerwine's requests. My sole obligation was to provide a deed and an accounting of my expenses once certified funds had been delivered to Stockgrowers State Bank. Why should I spend the money to survey the property and give Sowerwine an extension of time when he was not willing to discuss providing me with some sort of additional compensation as an inducement to do so?

I worked hand in glove with my attorneys, who I deemed extremely competent. We believed the case would be viewed by the judge as a nuisance suit and dismissed summarily. We were wrong. The case went to trial in June of 1983, and on August 29, 1983, Judge John T. Dixon ruled in favor of Sowerwine.

In his Judgment, Judge Dixon allowed the Sowerwines an additional four months to raise the money to repurchase the property, extending the amount of time from their original default for non-payment to more than a year and a half. He further ordered that if the Sowerwines were able to tender the repurchase monies within the extended time period, I had to deed the property back to them within five days. To add insult to injury, Judge Dixon ruled that if I refused to deed the property back to Sowerwine – as I might do pending an appeal – the court would execute a deed to Sowerwine on my behalf, and I would be denied the five acres and the profit that the contract with Sowerwine guaranteed me.

I did appeal the decision to the Wyoming Supreme Court, and consequently I did not execute the deed as ordered by Judge Dixon when Sowerwine deposited the repurchase monies at the designated bank on December 2, 1983. I wasn't about to deed the property to him before my appeal had been heard and ruled upon. As it turned out, the Wyoming Supreme Court upheld the lower court's decision. In 1985, they ruled that the lower court judge had the best opportunity to see and hear all the evidence and they refused to overturn his decision.

The consequences were devastating for me, emotionally and financially. It took several years for me to recover from that decision. I lost my money and I lost my pride. I vowed that would not happen again.

Stockton et al vs. Velasquez, and subsequently Rio Arriba County, NM (2003)

In 1997 my wife and I purchased 250 acres of land in north central New Mexico on which we planned to build our dream house. The land had once been incorporated within the Piedra Lumbre Land Grant, one of many private and communal land grants created by the King of Spain to facilitate settlement in the new world. The Piedra Lumbre Grant, originally containing nearly 50,000 acres, was a private grant given to Pedro Martin Serrano in 1766.

When the region became part of the United States at the end of the Mexican War, the status of the grant was upheld by the US government subsequent to the Treaty of Guadalupe Hidalgo, signed on February 2, 1848. It was determined that the grant was legitimate, and the owners could retain their lands, subject to the laws of the United States governing land ownership rights and responsibilities. Over the next hundred and fifty years the grant was divided among heirs and sold off. By the mid 1900s, Anglo-Americans began buying parcels of the land in significant numbers and building permanent homes. A segment of the Hispanic population began to take offense to the purchase of old grant lands by Anglos, and did their utmost to make life uncomfortable for the new owners.

In 1967, a group known locally as the Alianza (The Alliance) led by the activist Reies Tijerina met in the village of Coyote, only a few miles from where our home is now located. The state police alleged the meeting had been organized by agitators and ordered them to disband. When they refused, several members were arrested. Two days later, Tijerina led his men in a raid on the Rio Arriba County Courthouse in Tierra Amarilla to free the imprisoned members. In the process, a prison guard and a sheriff's deputy were shot, and two hostages were taken. A huge manhunt ensued, and Tijerina surrendered after only a few days on the run. He ultimately served just two years in federal prison for his involvement in the 1967 raid, but succeeded in bringing national attention to the land grant issue in northern New Mexico. One of Tijerina's followers on that June day in 1967 was a man named Uvaldo Velasquez.

In 2003, my wife and I encountered a "family reunion" of the Velasquez clan being held on our property. The intruders said that we had no proper claim to the property and that they, as Hispanics, had every right to enjoy the benefits of the land granted to Pedro Martin Serrano by the King of Spain. We politely disagreed and asked the folks – who numbered nearly 20 – to leave. They refused, and it quickly became apparent they were looking for a fight. Instead of taking the bait, we called local authorities (who proved useless), notified our attorney, and eventually filed a quiet title action along with neighboring landowners to avoid future encounters. We also asked the court to issue a restraining order against all members of the Velasquez family.

After many months and many court appearances, we received the satisfaction we sought. The court ruled that no parties had any legal right to our properties other than the owners of record, and a permanent restraining order was issued against all members of the Velasquez family.

At that point, however, the County of Rio Arriba jumped into the fray, claiming our private ranch road was a public county road by virtue of its historic use. Many of the county commissioners and administrators were sympathetic to the Velasquez cause, which was simply an extension of the cause promoted by the Alianza. After two tedious years at court, including one failed attempt at mediation, we prevailed. The court determined our ranch road was indeed a private road. The county, whose personnel had by now made it very plain that this was a land grant issue and not a road issue, appealed the judge's decision and made it clear that if they were unsuccessful at appeal they would move to have the road condemned. That case is ongoing.

<u>Evaluation Services, Inc. vs. Lender's Service, Inc. (2004)</u>

In 1981 I began developing what have become known as automated valuation models for real estate valuation. If you have ever seen the advertisement on television that focuses on a group of people hovering over a crystal ball and asks, "Do you know what your house is worth?"- well, I fathered that apparently mystifying technology. The process involves combining real estate information acquired from tax assessment offices and other sources with analytical computer programs (Software) to arrive at value estimates—all without ever visiting the properties being valued. The value estimates have proven to be quite accurate for the 70%+/- of those properties in the US that are relatively homogeneous. This method of valuing real property has revolutionized the real estate appraisal industry.

In the early 1990s, I formed a partnership with an individual who owned a well respected appraisal firm that conducted business throughout the State of Colorado. We implemented the Software in his offices and began producing automated valuations all along the Front Range in cities that included the Denver metropolitan area and Colorado Springs. Lenders loved our product and we made plans to expand our coverage within the State. At the same time, we created a new entity named Evaluation Services, Inc. (ESI) for the purpose of marketing the Software to a company having the size and resources to implement the valuation system nationwide. We found a willing buyer in an appraisal management company located in Pittsburgh, Pennsylvania, named Lender's Service, Inc. (LSI), a wholly owned subsidiary of Merrill Lynch. LSI was (and is, although under a new name) a company that managed the real estate appraisal processes for several of the nation's largest lenders, and they were the biggest such company in the country.

The sale to LSI was completed on September 30, 1997, with the execution of the following agreements:

- ✓ A Software Purchase Agreement that set forth the terms of the purchase and included a provision barring us from working in the automated valuation industry for anyone except LSI for a period of eight years (a covenant not to compete)

- ✓ A Consulting Agreement that obligated us to work for LSI in a consulting capacity for no less than three years
- ✓ A Lease Agreement that allowed us to use LSI's Pittsburgh offices while we helped them implement the Software
- ✓ Two identical Software License Agreements (one between ESI and LSI and the other between my partner's appraisal company, Willman & Associates, and LSI) that required LSI to return two copies of the Software to us so that we could continue our automated property valuation business in the State of Colorado.

Despite the promises contained in these agreements, LSI failed to fulfill all of their obligations. In order to quell the disputes that arose as a result of their lack of performance, LSI made more promises over the years and put them in writing in the form of amendments to existing agreements and, on occasion, new agreements. They failed to fulfill those promises as well.

After a rocky relationship that spanned half a dozen years, we filed suit in Allegheny County, Pennsylvania (Pittsburgh) in November of 2004. In our Complaint, we enumerated five claims against LSI, but we dropped three of those claims by the time of our pre-trial hearing in 2006. The two remaining claims were for lost profits pursuant to LSI's breach of the Software License Agreements. The agreements obligated LSI to provide us two copies of the Software and, as per subsequent amendments, access to their Internet-based valuation system so we could continue our ongoing property valuation business in Colorado. LSI breached both agreements; we never received the copies of the Software or the access to LSI's Internet-based system.

Without the Software (we were subject to a non-compete agreement that prevented us from purchasing or creating alternate software), we had to close the doors on our valuation business in Colorado.

LSI never denied their failure to perform. LSI instead sought protection from prosecution on the basis of three defenses:

1. We had failed to bring suit against LSI within four years of the contract breach, as required by the Pennsylvania Statute of Limitations, and
2. In 2002, we had executed a Settlement & Release Agreement wherein we promised not to sue LSI over grievances that had arisen prior to August 1, 2002, and
3. Our Software License Agreements contained Limitation on Liability provisions that barred us from suing for lost profits.

We asserted that we had not sued LSI earlier because each time we threatened suit – which we did with regularity – they offered to amend their original agreements and provide additional consideration in the form of money and/or services. Although the agreements were indeed amended (the one with ESI on two occasions, and the one with Willman & Associates on one occasion), LSI never lived up to the promises incorporated within those amendments. We contended that we were falsely induced to give LSI more time to perform, when their obvious intent had been to survive the statutory limitation period unscathed. We argued that because of LSI's actions we should not be bound by the four-year statutory filing period for initiating our suit. We further asserted that their breach with regard to the Software Licensing Agreements had actually occurred at the time LSI had failed to perform on the *final* amendment between LSI and ESI, executed in September of 2002, and that our suit –

filed in November of 2004 – was well within the four year limitation period.

With respect to the Settlement & Release Agreement, we argued that LSI had failed to give us the full consideration required by the Agreement (an increase in royalties and a release of our covenant not to compete). Consequently that agreement had died for lack of consideration and became unenforceable.

Finally, we argued that the Limitation on Liability provision prevented us from suing LSI for lost revenues resulting from "damages arising from or relating to ESI's use of the Software," as our agreement stated. We weren't suing for any damage resulting from the *use* of the Software; we were suing because we *never received* the Software and were therefore unable to continue our property valuation business in the State of Colorado.

LSI argued that our case had no merit and asked the Pennsylvania Court of Common Pleas to dismiss the case summarily, which they did in May of 2006. We subsequently filed an appeal with the Superior Court of Pennsylvania, asking that they reverse the lower court's decision and remand the case back to the Court of Common Pleas for trial. The Superior Court heard our argument in June of 2007 and on October 1, 2007 they issued their decision, ruling against us.

In January of 2008 we filed an appeal with the Supreme Court of Pennsylvania. Toward year end we received the court's ruling:

ORDER

AND NOW, this 1st day on October, 2008, the Petition for Allowance of Appeal is hereby DENIED.

After nearly four years of litigation, we were out of court, having never had an opportunity to be heard at trial.

Evaluation Services, Inc. vs. Lender's Service, Inc. (2006)

Among the agreements we executed with LSI when we sold them the Software in 1997 was a Consulting Agreement. Per the terms of that agreement, we agreed to work with LSI for three years to help them maintain, enhance and implement the Software.

As was the case with several of our agreements, the Consulting Agreement was extended by amendment on two occasions – once in September of 2000 and again on August 1, 2002. This final amendment incorporated a schedule of work to be completed within the first eight months following the amendment (by March 31, 2003). Both ESI and LSI had specific tasks to accomplish during the defined eight-month period. If we performed on time, regardless of LSI's performance, we were to be paid an incentive bonus and our covenant not to compete in the automated valuation industry, which we agreed to at the time of the sale in 1997, was to be immediately terminated. The agreement also contained an arbitration clause which provided that any dispute arising from non-performance by either party would be arbitrated rather than litigated.

On March 18, 2003 – prior to the end of the eight-month task period – we notified LSI that our work had been completed. We requested our bonus and the termination of the covenant not to compete. We also notified LSI that they had failed to perform *any* of the tasks required of them under the terms of the agreement.

LSI acknowledged that we had indeed completed all of our tasks to their satisfaction, and they paid our incentive bonus. They failed, however, to release us from our covenant not to compete. LSI's continual refusal to deliver the release contributed to our decision to take legal action in November of 2004.

We filed our demand for arbitration with respect to LSI's failure to perform under the terms of the Consulting Agreement, as amended, in September of 2006, well within the statutory period for such filings. LSI did not deny they had failed to comply with their obligations under the Consulting Agreement. Instead, they responded that we should be barred from arbitration because this claim had already been litigated; they said we had included the claim in our suit filed at Court in 2004. We denied that. We had used LSI's breach of the Consulting Agreement as one of several examples of LSI's bad faith conduct in another of our claims, Breach of the Covenant of Good Faith and Fair Dealing, but we had never made a claim against LSI for their breach of the Consulting Agreement. We couldn't; the amendment to the Consulting Agreement specified that disputes had to be arbitrated.

LSI filed a motion at Court in Pittsburgh to have us barred from arbitration in this matter, and on April 11, 2007 Judge Judith Friedman ruled in LSI's favor. Her court order specified that, "Defendant (ESI) is prohibited from continuing the arbitration proceeding that it initiated before the AAA (American Arbitration Association) and is hereby ordered to immediately terminate such proceedings."

We terminated our arbitration proceeding and immediately filed an appeal with the Pennsylvania Superior Court.

Our hearing on appeal was held March 18, 2008, and on June 6, 2008 the Superior Court upheld the lower court's decision in favor of LSI. In so doing, they created a legal precedent that is so illogical that I believe it will most certainly be overturned one day. In essence, they decided that a breach of contract is a breach of contract, and that the reason for the breach – be it inadvertent or intentional – is of no consequence.

We immediately filed an appeal with the Pennsylvania Supreme Court, but as with our primary case against LSI, the court denied our appeal. On November 17, 2008, we received their final order; both of our cases against LSI were over.

THE STRUCTURE OF OUR LEGAL SYSTEM

At the onset, it is important to point out that there are several alternatives available for dispute resolution in the United States. Of the millions of lawsuits filed each year, only a small fraction ever make it to court. The Bureau of Justice Statistics has reported that only perhaps 3% of all tort, contract and real property cases are resolved at trial. It is important that you know the options available to you.

<u>Settlement between the Parties</u>
There are occasions when differences can be settled by the parties through peaceful negotiation with or without an intermediary. Sometimes matters can be resolved through informal meetings, telephone conferences, or written correspondence.

A formal approach to negotiation is called mediation, which involves an impartial third-party mediator. In some states, mediation is a mandatory step in the litigation process. In those states, for certain types of cases the litigants might be obliged to attempt mediation after a lower court has handed down a ruling and before an appeal can be heard. There are benefits to all concerned if matters can be settled out of court. That being said, neither negotiation nor mediation is a binding process; any party can walk away from it at any time before a final agreement is reached.

Regardless of the nature of the dispute, it is my opinion that the settlement option should always be considered. It is pointless to subject yourself to the emotional and financial costs of going to court if there is a possibility that the disagreement might be resolved amicably through open discussion between the parties. I would, however, add a couple of caveats to that statement.

First, never threaten suit or bring suit against another with the intent of settling out of court. An attorney once told me that when he handles a case, nothing that transpires on the way to the courtroom is predicated on a desire to settle. If settlement occurs, that's fine, but he maintains that settlement should not be part of an overall strategy. His reasoning was simple:

- If you enter a suit with intent to settle, your motives appear (and probably are) insincere.
- If settlement is part of your strategy, you might fail to focus on the essential points that can dictate whether you win or lose at court.

I think he is correct.

Second, if you can resolve matters without litigation, make sure the new agreement between the parties is reduced to writing in a document that accurately and completely describes the new understanding. If this new agreement should fall apart and issues prove irreconcilable in the future, the document that defines your settlement terms might become extremely significant.

Example:

During the course of our involvement with LSI, there were numerous instances when we notified them they had breached one or more provisions of their contracts with us. On each occasion they asked us not to sue; they instead offered to amend the existing agreements, which would allow them an opportunity to comply and provide us additional compensation for our leniency. These negotiated settlements (amendments) made sense to us. It appeared we had nothing to lose and everything to gain by giving LSI time to comply, thus avoiding litigation.

We were ultimately forced to file suit after LSI failed to comply with the provisions of the amendments as well. At court, LSI claimed we should be barred from suing them because we had waited too long to file our claims. They said the Pennsylvania Statute of Limitations governing contracts precluded us from bringing a claim for breach of contract more than four years after the breach first occurred. This became a central point of contention during our litigation. If we had incorporated provisions into the amendments that spoke specifically to this matter – that the limitation period would begin anew as of the date of each new amendment – this issue would have been moot.

In addition to attempting to resolve matters with LSI through negotiation, my wife and I and our neighbors have been involved in formal mediation with Rio Arriba County. While the mediation was unsuccessful, it cost us nothing except time. However, I believe that satisfactory settlement in both cases would have been possible if the opposing parties had been sincere about their efforts to negotiate reasonable solutions. If the negotiations had been successful, the time spent would have been a welcome investment when compared to the eventual cost of litigation.

Arbitration

Arbitration is a means of dispute resolution that has been established outside of the court system where parties refer their dispute to one or more arbitrators whose decision is legally binding upon the parties. Although there is a non-binding type of arbitration as well (usually taking the form of mediation), I refer here to binding arbitration only.

In an effort to standardize the arbitration process, the Uniform Arbitration Act was created many years ago and has since been adopted by all 50 states. Subsequent to its adoption several private organizations have been created to administer arbitration proceedings. The American Arbitration Association (AAA) is one of these, and is often cited in agreements between parties as the administrator in the event of a dispute.

Parties can agree to arbitrate rather than litigate at any time, but it is best to elect that option at the time an agreement is being negotiated rather than after a dispute has arisen. Once a disagreement occurs, it is often difficult to find common ground on any issue related to the matter. An arbitration provision in an agreement usually sets forth the intent of the parties to use arbitration as the means of dispute resolution, identifies how the arbitration will be administered, and who shall bear the costs of the arbitration. The administrator will, in turn, prescribe the procedure for the selection of the arbitrator and the prosecution of the dispute. The resulting decision of the arbitrator will be binding on the parties; however, the ability to appeal a decision at court is available to the parties just as it would have been had the matter been litigated.

As with everything else in life and business, there are pluses and minuses to arbitration. On the plus side, arbitration often takes less time than litigation, and the cost is generally much less as well. While the process mimics the litigation process, it is more informal (generally requires fewer filings and hearings) and more abbreviated (limited testimony, etc.).

On the negative side, the decision will be rendered by a single individual or panel of individuals – the arbitrator(s). Arbitrators can be, but are not necessarily, lawyers. While this can be viewed as a minus, it could also be viewed as a plus. Depending upon the legal complexities of a case, a good arbitrator is capable of forming prudent decisions based on the evidence and the circumstances as well as any judge, and perhaps better. Arbitrators are often less politically motivated and less dependent on any given constituency for their positions as intermediaries.

If the agreement of the parties is not complicated, if the intent of the parties is clear, and if there are few contingencies that can affect the interpretation of the agreement, arbitration should be considered as a means of dispute resolution.

Courts

If neither settlement nor arbitration is possible or appropriate, the only remaining alternative is to litigate (dueling was outlawed years ago). Our nation's court system is divided into state and federal courts, although there may be local (municipal) courts authorized within states, as well. Not every court has the authority to hear any individual case. Cases that individuals are likely to be involved in (divorce, breach of contract, traffic violation) are usually heard at state court. Federal courts generally hear cases that deal with constitutional law, cases in which the federal government is a party, and special issues like bankruptcy, patent infringement or cases involving maritime law.

There are circumstances where parties have the right to choose to have their case heard by either a state or federal court; if the parties reside in different states and the amount of relief being sought exceeds $75,000, the Plaintiff may file suit in either court.

When we filed suit against LSI in 2004, we had to decide whether we wanted to file in state or federal court. LSI was a Delaware corporation located in Pennsylvania and Evaluation Services, Inc. was a Wyoming corporation. We were seeking damages well in excess of the statutory $75,000, so we were allowed to file in either jurisdiction. We pondered where we might have the best opportunity of winning our case, and compiled a mental list of Pros and Cons that looked something like this:

Pro State:	Our case would probably be heard more quickly at state court
Pro State:	Our attorney had more experience with, and knowledge of, the state court system in Pennsylvania
Pro Federal:	LSI might be politically connected in Pennsylvania, and might use that to their advantage
Pro Federal:	A jury (or a judge) in Pennsylvania might be sympathetic to a large local employer
Neutral:	We had no reason to believe that judges at either level would be better educated or more apt to give our case the consideration it deserved

We decided to file our case at state court primarily because we (our attorney included) were less familiar with federal court, and we had no reason to believe we would not be afforded a fair hearing in either venue.

In retrospect, was that a prudent decision? I think so. I don't believe we received a fair hearing before the Court in Pittsburgh, or the Pennsylvania Superior Court, for that matter. However, I can't say we would have had a fair hearing at federal court either. I don't believe you can approach pending litigation with the idea that the system will be anything but fair and just. You have to take every precaution to protect yourself, but if you're preoccupied by the specter of conspiracy or impropriety, you probably don't have the personal constitution that litigation requires.

At Court we had yet another decision to make. We could opt to have a trial by jury or a bench trial, which is essentially the same as a jury trial only without the jury. At a bench trial a judge hears the case and renders the decision. There are pros and cons to both these options as well. When we sued LSI, we originally requested a trial by jury. However, we dropped that request during our pre-trial hearing in April of 2006 for reasons that will be explained later on in this text.

Jury trials can, on occasion, take more time and become more costly than bench trials. Since a judge is presumably familiar with the law, less time might be required during a bench trial to explain legal nuances and prove damages. The list of witnesses in a bench trial might be able to be pared to only those whose testimony is most relevant. Again, one would reasonably presume that a judge would require less information to make a sound decision than would a panel of ordinary citizens who are unfamiliar with the legal system and require more elaborate explanation.

In my case against Sowerwine, his attorney had requested a jury trial in the Complaint filed in September of 1982. We, believing that the judge presiding over the 5th Judicial District in Wyoming (Judge Dixon) was well acquainted with Sowerwine and his shenanigans, filed a motion in March of 1983 to strike Sowerwine's jury demand. We were successful. In April of 1983 Judge Dixon ordered that the matter would be tried before the court without a jury. In retrospect, that might have been a mistake on our part. I might have had better fortune before a jury of my peers.

This brings into play the entire issue of whether you might profit from being judged by a panel of your peers rather than one individual who, though well versed in legal matters, is certainly not infallible. This topic will be dealt with in some detail later on.

THE PROCESS OF LITIGATION

The actual process of litigation doesn't necessarily follow a straight and narrow path. A court case can, and often does, take many unexpected twists and turns. However, whether the case involves personal injury, breach of contract or any of a multitude of civil claims, the basic steps in a lawsuit might be described as follows:

- The Plaintiff (the person with the complaint) sends a demand letter to the Defendant (the person defending against the complaint) expressing certain grievances and demanding some sort of specific satisfaction (action, money, etc.)
- The Defendant either fails to respond to the demand letter, or rejects it.
- The Plaintiff files a Complaint in the appropriate jurisdiction (State District Court, Federal Court).
- Notice of the formal Complaint is served on the Defendant(s).
- The Defendant files a formal response to the Complaint, and possibly a counterclaim (a Complaint against the Plaintiff).
- Defendant files preliminary objections asking the court to dismiss the case on the basis of legal insufficiency, or some such reasoning.
- The parties enter Discovery – the period during which the facts of the case are disclosed between the parties. Discovery might include:
    - Interrogatories – a list of questions exchanged between the parties that must be answered truthfully and returned

  - Depositions – question-and-answer session performed under oath, in the presence of a court reporter (may include parties to the suit and/or witnesses anticipated by the suit)
  - Request for documents – exchange of pertinent documents between the parties
  - Disclosure of expert witnesses – the parties reveal to one another the names of any expert witnesses they might use in the course of the trial
- Filing of miscellaneous motions to force compliance with discovery, to request a hearing for summary judgment (dismissal of the case based on lack of adequate evidence), etc.
- Trial date is established.
- Pretrial hearing during which a judge determines if there is any basis for settlement and, if not, whether all documents and filings are in order so the case can proceed to trial
- Trial by judge or by jury
  - Opening statements
  - Testimony of witnesses
    - Cross examination
  - Presentation of evidence
  - Closing statements
- A verdict is rendered by the jury or the judge
  - If a bench trial, the judge's decision might not be forthcoming for weeks or months
- Post trial motions (motion for clarification, motion for reconsideration)
- Appeal of the decision

The process, start to finish (excluding any appeal), can be expected to take from one to two years.

COMMON PERCEPTIONS AND MISCONCEPTIONS

Many of us think we have some idea of what we might expect if and when faced with litigation, whether we are the party bringing suit or the one defending our actions. We may soon realize that many of our perceptions are in truth misconceptions. Here are some aspects of our legal system that you might ponder now, before you find yourself in court. They aren't meant to discourage you, but rather to enlighten you. They speak to common misconceptions that you need to be aware of so that you can make prudent decisions.

<u>Misconception</u>: *Your attorney can and will handle procedural matters. You don't have to be concerned with them.*

<u>Advice</u>: *Pay close attention to procedural matters.*

My introduction to the litigation process began in 1982 during my lawsuit with the Sowerwine family. From day one, I knew I had not violated either the terms of our contract or the spirit of our agreement, so I was positively confident of the outcome. Despite my confidence, I went to some lengths to insure success. In addition to my local counsel, I retained the services of a prominent trial lawyer. I also asked several other attorneys with whom I was personally acquainted to review the case and give me their advice. With the exception of one individual, the lawyers concluded that the suit was frivolous and the court would dismiss the case prior to trial. The lone attorney who offered a differing view cautioned that the court might interpret the transaction as a mortgage – my purchase being akin to a loan that could be repaid by means of the repurchase within the twelve-month period. In the event a court construed the agreement as being a mortgage, I might have to provide Sowerwine a redemption period during which he could continue to seek alternate funding to buy back the land. Regardless, the worst case presented to me was that I might incur additional carrying costs, but at the end of the day I would either retain the property or be compensated as per the terms of the agreement.

I spent a good deal of time over the course of the next year documenting the negotiations and conversations that led up to our 1981 agreement, and working closely with counsel. I focused on the particulars of the purchase and paid little attention to procedural matters of court. I believed that the factual, substantive issues were what had import – not necessarily matters of procedure. I left those issues up to my attorneys.

In retrospect, although I thought I was deeply invested in the case at the time, I was completely out of the loop as far as procedural matters were concerned. That was my choice and should not reflect poorly on my counsel. To be honest, the procedural issues confused me, and I thought decisions pertaining to the actual trial process were best left to the discretion of my attorneys. I realize now that I should have become much more involved in procedural issues.

By way of example, there were two procedural issues that had an immense impact on the Sowerwine case at trial, and I remained silent on both. The first was a statement made by Judge Dixon at the very onset of the trial. E.O. Sowerwine, Jr. had appeared before the judge on several previous occasions, and a mutual animosity had developed between the two. Consequently, Judge Dixon had developed a stance of "no tolerance" toward Sowerwine, and he stated that E.O. Sowerwine, Jr. (the father) would not be allowed in his courtroom during the trial. He further stated that if we had a problem with that, we should petition for a different judge to preside over the trial. My attorney agreed to the judge's conditions and said we would proceed. Had I been wiser, I might have objected. I might have asked my attorney to accept the judge's offer to petition the court for an alternate judge.

Papa (as I came to call him) Sowerwine's lack of credibility was central to our defense; his creditworthiness and his character had to be attacked at trial. It would be virtually impossible to do that effectively without Sowerwine personally in attendance. However, I must admit that upon hearing the Judge Dixon's statement regarding Sowerwine I developed a false sense of comfort. I thought the judge must know and understand the frivolous nature of the suit if he understood the unorthodox nature of Sowerwine himself. That initial reaction conflicted with a visceral consciousness that this was an important matter and that my attorney and I should consider it carefully. If faced with the same situation today, I would ask my attorney to request a brief recess so we could discuss the pros and cons of the subject.

The second procedural issue that had a significant impact on the case also arose on the first day of the trial. In his opening statement, Judge Dixon said the trial would end Friday afternoon regardless of whether the attorney for the plaintiff and the attorney for the defense had finished presenting their respective cases. The judge had to be somewhere the following Monday, and he wasn't going to carry the case over for continuation after his return. I didn't know whether the time restraint imposed by the judge was reasonable or unreasonable, so I didn't speak up. Both attorneys agreed to the judge's condition.

As it turned out, we modified our presentation to accommodate the time limitation, and we still never got to final arguments before the end of day on Friday. Consequently, the judge stated that final arguments would be submitted in writing on or before a future date of his choosing. My attorney submitted our final argument well in advance of the deadline, and defense counsel, with the benefit of our filed argument in hand, responded with a splendid story that was part rebuttal and part fiction. The judge's ruling, issued several months later, went against us and in favor of the defense – and followed the story line Sowerwine's attorney had penned point by point.

I ran into Sowerwine's attorney at a social function months later, and he made the comment that he had been handed an unbelievable opportunity to fashion his final argument in a winning manner by virtue of the timing of these closing events. If I had known then what I know now, I would have parleyed with my counsel when the judge initially established the time limit, and I would have argued against the condition even if it meant delaying the trial.

As I reflect upon these things, I remember that at the time I was anxious to get on with the trial at almost any cost. The time and money I had invested in the case had been much more burdensome than I had originally anticipated, and I wanted the trial to be over. I had always assumed I would prevail, so a delay for any reason seemed senseless. I would now give serious consideration to the impact of these types of issues and exercise more patience – as difficult as that might be.

I also would advise anyone faced with a similar situation (unusual as it might be) to wait to file their final argument until very near the filing deadline. There is nothing to be gained – and perhaps much to be lost – by filing so early that the opposition might benefit from reading the document before preparing their own.

When I look back on all this today, I wonder if Judge Dixon wasn't trying to encourage us to take our case before a different judge. Had I been more perceptive, I might have come to that conclusion. I wonder now how that might have affected the outcome of the case.

<u>Misconception</u>: *Law equals justice.*
<u>Advice</u>: *The law is not necessarily just. It is just the law.*

The first time I became involved in litigation (the Sowerwine suit), I was livid. When I was notified by my attorneys that they had received notice of suit against me, I was defiant. I had adhered to our agreement; I had purchased the land and satisfied all of Sowerwine's creditors. I was not required to do anything else unless Sowerwine tendered the repurchase monies on or before the deadline, at the designated banking institution. He failed to do that and was claiming that I was the cause of his failure. I wasn't. I said "I'm in the right. Let him sue me."

It was then that one of the attorneys present told me a story that has been told and retold in legal circles for generations.

A first-year law student had been listening to a lecture by his professor regarding a point of law that seemed contrary to everything the young man's parents had taught him about right and wrong. After a short time he could no longer contain himself. He raised his hand and when called upon said, "But that isn't right. Clearly, what you have told us leads to an unjust conclusion." In response, the professor asked the student to walk outside, read the inscription over the door to the building, return and tell the class what it said. After a minute or two, the young man returned and stated that the inscription said "School of Law." The professor asked, "Does it say the School of Right and Wrong?" whereupon the young man said, "No, it doesn't." The professor then asked, "Does it say the School of Justice?", and again the young man said, "No." The professor addressed the entire class saying, "This is the School of Law, not the School of Right and Wrong nor the School of Justice. Don't ever forget that."

I, for one, have never forgotten that. What happens in a courtroom might seem just and it might seem right, but it is every bit as likely that it will seem wrong or unjust. What goes on in the courtroom is governed by the laws of the land as interpreted in connection with a specific set of circumstances, and the outcome may have little relevance to right and wrong. As unimaginable as that might sound, it is correct. Let me give you an example.

In my 2004 case with LSI, two things were to happen on September 30, 1997, the day LSI officially purchased the Software from our company. The Software, one copy of which had previously been escrowed (all remaining copies had been destroyed as per the instructions of LSI's counsel), was to be delivered to LSI for authentication and verification after which LSI was to hand me a check for the initial payment along with two copies of the Software for use in our existing valuation business in Colorado. They took possession of and validated the Software. They gave me a check, but failed to deliver any copy of the Software. It was after business hours by the time I received the check, and it was therefore too late in the day for LSI to duplicate the Software for me. I wasn't terribly concerned; I knew I would be returning to Pittsburgh to begin my consulting duties within a few weeks. I would get the Software then.

Once my partner and I returned to Pittsburgh, LSI continued to drag their feet regarding the delivery of the Software. They said they would get it to us when they found time to make the copies, and told us to cool our heels. We were reluctant to push too hard, because our relationship with LSI was such that we were reliant upon them for much more than the delivery of the Software. They still owed us Software payments, they owed us Software royalties, we were bound to them by consulting contracts, and we had agreed not to work in the automated valuation industry for anyone except LSI until the fall of 2005 (with the exception that we could continue our valuation business in Colorado). Our relationship with LSI was broad and exclusive, and we were hesitant to damage the association for this single cause. We decided it would be in our best interest to try everything *but* litigation.

When finally LSI's inaction became untenable, we threatened suit. They told us legal action would not be necessary; they offered to amend the Software License Agreements, promising to give us access to their Internet version of the system in addition to delivering the Software as they were already required to do, if we would give them a couple of additional months to fulfill the obligations. We agreed to their resolution, and in September of 2000 we executed amendments to the original Agreements that incorporated these new promises.

Once again LSI failed and refused to perform. They did not deliver the Software and they did not give us access to their Internet valuation system. When we again threatened suit, they offered yet another amendment with a new deadline for their performance. By this time there had been a change in management at LSI and the new CEO assured us his team was more honorable than the group they had replaced. Another round of amendments was signed in the autumn of 2002. When LSI failed to perform on these contractual obligations, we filed suit.

We filed our suit in November of 2004, after attempting – without success – to mediate the matter over a period of several months. In 2006, pursuant to a hearing on Summary Judgment (a hearing to dismiss the case), the Court of Common Pleas in Pittsburgh, Pennsylvania ruled that we were barred from suing LSI for their failure to deliver the Software. The Court decided that, although LSI had indeed breached their contract(s) with us, we had failed to file suit on a timely basis. The Court said the breach had first occurred when LSI failed to deliver the Software on September 30, 1997. Since the State of Pennsylvania has a statutory limit on the time during which a suit can be filed following a breach of contact (4 years), and since we had failed to initiated suit within the appropriate time period, the Court determined that we had forfeited our right to sue.

We filed an appeal with the Superior Court of Pennsylvania in which we argued that the breach that was the subject of our Complaint did not occur on September 30, 1997. The Software License Agreements did not specify a delivery date for the Software. They simply spoke to our right to use "the accompanying copy of the Software." This implied LSI was to deliver the Software concurrent with the execution of the Software License Agreements, but there was no date certain. The amendments to the License Agreements in 2000 and 2002 contained the identical verbiage. We emphasized that the court did not have the right to impose or imply a specific delivery date when no such date existed. We maintained that the breach we referred to in our suit occurred at the time LSI failed to perform following the last amendment to the original agreement, which was executed in September of 2002. That amendment had been executed *after* the supposed statutory four-year term had expired. There was nothing contained in the amendment that modified LSI's original obligation to deliver the Software, and it retained the reference to "the accompanying copy of the Software." We postulated that had LSI's obligation lapsed prior to the execution of this amendment due to a statute of limitation, certainly LSI would have included something in the amendment that indicated they were no longer liable for the delivery of the Software. In addition, we provided the court with written correspondence from LSI's CEO dated in January of 2002 – once again after the supposed statutory four year term had expired – in which he acknowledged LSI's obligation to deliver the Software, and expressed his intent to forward a copy to us (although he never did).

The Superior Court agreed with the decision of the lower Court in favor of LSI. This was the Superior Court's rationale:

The breach occurred on September 30, 1997. The amendments, while reaffirming all obligations under the original agreement, did not establish a new and later delivery date for the Software. The delivery date, therefore, remained September 30, 1997, and was simply reaffirmed as such. The statutory period for the filing of our claim therefore expired four years from that date, on September 30, 2001 – despite the amendments executed in 2000 and 2002.

It seemed interesting to me then – as it does now – that these pillars of wisdom and knowledge would determine that the language in the agreement executed *after* the expiration of the statutory limitation period on September 30, 2001 would reaffirm an obligation that was no longer an obligation. Difficult logic to understand.

The fact that LSI had induced us to drop our threats of litigation in 2000 and again in 2002 by promising performance and then ignoring their promises, was apparently lost on the Court. Relying on the Superior Court's interpretation, LSI in essence persuaded us not to sue them during the statutory period by making false contractual promises, and after the statutory period expired, claimed immunity from prosecution on the grounds that we had waited too long to bring suit. That's a tidy way to avoid contractual responsibility, and the Courts – both the Allegheny County Court of Common Pleas and the Pennsylvania Superior Court, and eventually the Supreme Court of Pennsylvania – let LSI get away with it.

We found the Courts' interpretations interesting. I don't buy their rationale, and I think it's wrong. I believe the Courts allowed LSI to manipulate the letter of the law to defeat the intent of the law. The result was a court decision that – although based on law – was, in my opinion, unjust.

By the way, if there is a moral to this tale, it is this:

If you feel you are being treated unjustly and that you should sue, don't let anyone talk you out of it by promising action. Demand action and if it is not immediately forthcoming, sue.

Misconception: *Venue and governing law are unimportant.*
Advice: *Both might be extremely important.*

There is a difference between "venue" and "governing law." Venue is the place where a case is heard. Governing Law is the law that will be applied, regardless of where the case is heard. If you have entered into an agreement that has a Governing Law provision, and if a dispute erupts between the parties and litigation is pursued, the case will be subject to the state law specified in the agreement, regardless of where that case is heard (the "venue").

My first introduction to litigation occurred when I lived in Park County, Wyoming. The Sowerwine family who was taking me to court also lived in Park County, Wyoming. Venue was not an issue; the proceedings were held in Park County, Wyoming.

When we entered into our original Purchase Agreement with Lender's Service, Inc. it was established by agreement of the parties that should any disagreements arise, "This Agreement shall be governed by and construed in accordance with the laws of the Commonwealth of Pennsylvania." I didn't give that a great deal of thought at the time. I realized that in the event of a dispute, I might be forced to travel to Pennsylvania to argue on my behalf, and I would probably have to hire an attorney licensed to practice law in the Commonwealth of Pennsylvania. No big deal – I didn't expect to have any disputes with LSI back in September of 1997.

That all changed in 2004 when we filed our suit against LSI in the Court of Common Pleas, Allegheny County, Pennsylvania.

As previously mentioned, Pennsylvania has a four-year limitation on the period of time between which a contract breach occurs and the time a Plaintiff can bring suit for the breach. LSI's failure to deliver the Software to us in accordance with the terms of the Software License Agreements first occurred on September 30, 1997. When we threatened to take them to court over their failure to perform, LSI induced us to forgo litigation by offering to amend the Software License Agreements, promising access to their Internet based valuation system in addition to the delivery of the Software. They did this in the year 2000 and again in the year 2002. It was our contention that the period of limitation should have commenced only after LSI failed to perform subsequent to the amendment executed by the parties in September of 2002. At court, we argued that our suit, filed in November of 2004, was well within the limitation period.

Interestingly, this particular situation had never before been argued in a Pennsylvania courtroom, or at least there was no case law of record pertaining to such a situation. This specific circumstance combined inducement to forgo litigation with contractual amendments designed to provide additional compensation without disturbing the existing provisions of the original agreement. It was our assertion that, although LSI might have initially breached the Agreement on September 30, 1997, their statutory obligation had been extended by virtue of the amendments executed in 2000 and in 2002. We had initiated suit against LSI well within the four-year limitation period following LSI's final contractual promise – the 2002 amendment.

There were no Pennsylvania court decisions that provided precedent for our assertion that the Statute of Limitation did not bar us from bringing suit in this circumstance. There was, however, a similar case that had been argued in the neighboring State of Ohio in 1984 (Invacare Corp. vs. Sperry Corp.) where the judge decided:

"Fairness dictates that the most appropriate time to commence the running of the period of limitations is the date of the final supplemental contract."

The courts in Pennsylvania didn't buy this argument. Instead, they chose to bar us from suing LSI over this issue, contending the limitation period began on September 30, 1997 and was not affected by subsequent amendments and promises made by LSI.

An Ohio court might have seen this differently. At this point, both venue and governing law became very significant factors in our case.

What I had failed to realize was that laws vary from state to state, as do interpretations of basic legal tenets. When you enter into a contract and give your consent that the agreement shall be governed by and construed in accordance with the laws of a particular state, stop to consider what that means. I don't imply that you should be familiar with the laws of each state before you enter into an agreement. However, some states are known for their narrow interpretation of legal tenets, and others take a broader view of things.

Likewise, before you enter into a lawsuit, take some time to research case law and legal precedent in the state where the suit is to be litigated. Try to determine how the courts of that state have interpreted the law in situations similar to yours. A little bit of research at the start might help you decide how to frame your complaint, or how to respond to a complaint from another party.

People, since the beginning of time, have understood that the location of the field of battle sometimes gives one party an advantage over another. Take the high moral ground if you choose, but don't ignore the literal field of battle; that might prove to be far more important. Major General George Pickett's ill-fated charge at the Battle of Gettysburg on July

3, 1863 comes to mind. On that day, General Pickett was one of three Confederate generals who led a frontal assault across open ground against the Union army entrenched atop Cemetery and Seminary Ridges. Pickett's division was decimated, losing nearly twice the number of men killed, wounded or captured on the entire Union side that day.

The field of battle often favors one party over another, and that is worth remembering.

Most contractual agreements have Governing Law provisions, and often (but less frequently) the actual venue or forum for litigation is specified. Ask your attorney's advice on both of these matters. It might save you some money, and it might save your bacon.

Misconception: *You have a right to trial by a jury of your peers.*

Advice: *You are not guaranteed a trial, either by jury or by a judge.*

The Right to a Fair Trial

U.S. Supreme Court Chief Justice William Howard Taft (yes, the same individual who served as 27th President of the United States) made the comment in 1926 that "the real practical blessing of our Bill of Rights is in its provision for fixed procedure securing a fair hearing by independent courts to each individual." In fact, the Seventh Amendment to the US Constitution, which was part of the Bill of Rights adopted in 1791, reads as follows:

Amendment VII

Rights in civil cases

In Suits at common law, where the value in controversy shall exceed twenty dollars, the right of trial by jury shall be preserved, and no fact tried by a jury shall be otherwise re-examined in any Court of the United States, than according to the rules of the common law.

Thus, as most of us have long assumed, our Constitution guarantees us our day in court. In civil matters as in criminal matters, we are all entitled to a fair trial.

That's the perception, but is it an illusion?

When we filed our suit against LSI in November of 2004, we anticipated having a jury trial. That is indeed what we requested in our filings. For reasons explained later in this text, we decided to waive our right to a jury trial at the pre-trial hearing held in late April of 2006. We opted to have a "bench trial," a trial before a judge rather than before a jury.

My general impression was that a bench trial is basically the same as a jury trial – only without the jury. I assumed that the two options were much the same procedurally. And they are. However, with a bench trial the judge is given much more leeway to make decisions, and that presumably is a good thing; that's one reason why parties choose the bench trial option over a trial by jury.

What I was also aware of, but less concerned about, was that a judge might abuse this additional power to predetermine the outcome of the proceeding.

In the months leading up to our trial, before the pre-trial hearing in April of 2006, LSI had tried on three previous occasions to get the case thrown out of court. They had filed Preliminary Objections, a Motion to Stay Proceedings, and a Motion for Summary Judgment – all designed to encourage the court to dismiss our suit without ever going to trial.

Preliminary Objections:

LSI asked the court to throw the entire case out "on the ground of legal insufficiency." The motion was denied by Judge O'Reilly on August 2, 2005.

Motion to Stay Proceedings Pending Mediation:

LSI attempted to bar us from going to court in favor of mediating the issues subject to dispute. We had tried mediation and negotiation for nearly a year before filing suit and were not inclined to spend any additional time negotiating with a party whose intentions were clearly not sincere. The motion was denied on February 13, 2006 by Judge Strassburger.

Motion for Summary Judgment:

LSI asked the court to dismiss our case against them because they declared:

- ✓ We had failed to bring suit against LSI within four years of the contract breach, as required by the Pennsylvania Statute of Limitations, and
- ✓ In 2002, we had executed a Settlement & Release Agreement wherein we promised not to sue LSI over grievances that had arisen prior to August 1, 2002, and
- ✓ Our Software License Agreements contained Limitation on Liability provisions that barred us from suing for lost profits.

The Motion for Summary Judgment was denied by Judge Strassburger on April 20, 2006 and again by Judge Scanlon on May 1st.

The judges who ruled on these motions acknowledged that there were questions of fact that had to be dealt with, and they wisely ruled against LSI and in favor of proceeding to trial.

On May 3rd, 2006 – one week before our trial was to begin – LSI filed another motion asking the court to give them more time to prepare for trial. They filed the request with the scheduling judge, Judge Eugene Strassburger. Surprisingly, on May 4th Judge Strassburger not only granted LSI's request to delay the trial, but he also granted LSI a hearing on their Motion for Summary Judgment, filed on April 5th and denied by Judge Strassburger himself on April 20th. The exact same motion had also been denied by the trial judge, Judge Scanlon, on May 1st.

No Motion for Summary Judgment had even been presented to Judge Strassburger on May 3rd, and no new information had been entered for the court to consider. By ruling as he did, Judge Strassburger had made a court decision on a motion that had not been presented for his consideration, and one that both he and his fellow judge had denied within the preceding two weeks.

That ruling set a new chain of events in motion. We filed a complaint at Court claiming that Judge Strassburger had overstepped his authority. Judge Wettick, who was Judge Strassburger's superior, would not even entertain the complaint. Next, we presented Judge Strassburger with a formal motion asking him to reconsider his order. He would not.

The Hearing on Motion for Summary Judgment was held at the Allegheny County, Pennsylvania courthouse on June 12th, with Judge Scanlon presiding. Despite the fact that Scanlon had denied LSI's Motion for Summary Judgment on a prior occasion, at this hearing he ruled in favor of LSI. We were out of court, and left with no recourse but to appeal the decision to the Pennsylvania Superior Court.

Can't happen? Well, it did, and there went our guaranteed "day in court."

Would this have turned out differently had we not waived our right to a jury trial? I don't think so and neither did my counsel; we never got that far in the process. Was there something we could have done to protect against this outcome? Again, I don't believe there was. Our court system allows judges to dismiss cases for legal insufficiency or for lack of factual evidence, prior to trial. A judge must be able to provide a reason for dismissal if asked, but in the final analysis it is strictly a judgment call. Without this authority, court calendars would be clogged with cases that are frivolous and undeserving of the courts' time. The same authority that is designed to expedite the legal process does, however, open the door for impropriety if applied carelessly. Surely, the number of individuals who believe, as I do, that they have been robbed of their day in court by a judge who has made an ill-informed decision is enormous.

Let me explain why we decided to waive our right to a jury trial in this case. You might be faced with the same decision one day.

A Jury of Your Peers

We have all heard the phrase "a jury of our peers." Until I was confronted with the probability that I might face such a panel, I had never really considered what a jury of my peers might look like.

Evaluation Services, Inc. vs. Lender's Service, Inc. (2004)

I was born and raised in a middle-class family in Kansas City, the son of a physician and his wife. I attended a private boys' school from kindergarten through high school and went on to a rather inglorious college career, failing to finish. I moved west to Wyoming as a young lad and have lived all but two of my years since then in the West. Those two years were spent in Pittsburgh, Pennsylvania assisting LSI with the implementation of the Software they purchased from us in 1997. In 2004, when we filed our case against LSI, I was nearly 60 years old, a white Protestant male of upper middle class means.

As previously noted, it was agreed that our contracts with LSI would be governed by and construed in accordance with the laws of the Commonwealth of Pennsylvania. Consequently, when disputes arose, I faced the prospect of going to court in Pittsburgh. It didn't take me long to realize that the men and women who would sit in judgment on my case would, in all probability, have very little in common with me.

The census for Pittsburgh as of the year 2000 reveals that 33% of the population was non-white. Roughly half had some college education; 20% had never completed high school. The median household income was slightly more than $28,000 and approximately 4.2% of the population was unemployed. Nearly 95% of those employed worked for a wage or salary; fewer than 5% were self employed as was I. Fewer than 4% of the workers earned as much as I did on an annual basis.

I pondered these statistics and tried to visualize what my 12 jurors might look like. Based simply on the numbers, 9 of the 12 might be white, and 7 of the 12 would probably be women. While 6 might have had some college experience, it is likely that 3 would have failed to complete high school. Probably none would be self employed; probably all would earn less than I did annually. Considerably less. I came to the conclusion that my peers might not be able to relate to me. In fact, they might view me as odd or "foreign."

LSI, on the other hand, was a local company that employed several hundred people from the area. Following the demise of the steel industry in Pittsburgh and the subsequent rise in unemployment, any employer was looked upon with favor. Instead of being viewed as the big bad company taking advantage of the small businessman, I feared the jurors' sympathies might actually lean LSI's direction. That revelation surprised me. I had initially taken it for granted that LSI would be considered a Goliath against a poor defenseless David, and their seedy business practices designed to defraud a helpless independent businessman would be apparent. Now I wasn't so sure.

I questioned whether the jurors would be able to understand the issues well enough to avoid being schmoozed by some silver-tongued attorney representing our opponent. I worried that one vocal dissenter in a jury of 12 people might derail my case – and that began to appear quite likely.

After much consideration, we decided to forgo a jury trial and present our case before our trial judge. We felt the judge could easily grasp the legal issues and would be less apt to allow opposing counsel to confuse him with irrelevant issues.

Stockton et al vs. Velasquez (2003)

We never contemplated a jury trial in our case against the Velasquez family. We and our neighbors live in Rio Arriba County, New Mexico. A large rural county consisting of more than 5,850 square miles, it is home to only about 41,000 people. More than 70% of the residents are Hispanic. We and our neighbors fall within the 14% of people who are white, non-Hispanics. Although my wife and I still work full time, as do our neighbors, we are somehow viewed as belonging to a "privileged" class. In short, we are often made to feel unwelcome in a community where leaders are not reluctant to stand up in public meetings and openly discuss the need to bar Anglos from being able to purchase property in Rio Arriba County.

Our quiet title action against the Velasquez family and friends took nearly two years, and was heard before Judge Timothy Garcia at the Rio Arriba County courthouse in Tierra Amarilla, New Mexico. It took that long because Judge Garcia gave the Velasquez family more than their fair share of opportunities to provide the court with substantive information to support their claim that they had some right to our property. I will add that there had been two prior quiet title actions dealing with the exact same land in previous years, both of which involved Uvaldo Velasquez. This action had been required only because the number of defendants had been expanded to include individuals not named in prior litigation. The court had ruled against Mr. Velasquez on both previous occasions, and it was somewhat perplexing to us that we should even need to defend our title once again. Regardless, after many excruciating hearings held over a period of many months, we finally prevailed. However, the victory was bitter sweet. Before closing the book on the case, Judge Garcia told the Velasquez family in open court that they were no longer allowed to trespass on our property, "unless the county joins in the suit and can successfully prove that the Plaintiffs' road is a county road." Having provided the family the blueprint to continue their fight, Judge Garcia stepped aside "for personal reasons."

At the request of the Velasquez family, the county did in fact enter the battle, claiming that the road was and always had been a county road. They further asserted that if it wasn't a county road it should be because it had a history of use by locals who traversed our lands to cut firewood, hunt and recreate.

The litigation continued for another year before Judge Hall heard the case at trial in January of 2007. Trial lasted five days. Clear and convincing evidence was offered that proved the county had not constructed the road (we had), nor had they ever maintained the road – this despite the fact the county had been collecting funds from the State of New Mexico for many years as reimbursement for their cost of maintaining the road. Neither could the county provide any evidence that any road across our properties had been used without the knowledge and consent of the land owners for half a century; historic use was ruled out. Eleven months after the trial – which we believe was designed to be a "cooling off period" – Judge Hall ruled against the county and acknowledged that our road is definitely a private road. The Anglo judge's decision did not sit well with several Rio Arriba County commissioners who are not accustomed to being defied. The County filed an appeal and expressed their intent to begin condemnation proceedings should their appeal fail. They made no attempt to hide the fact that their efforts had little or nothing to do with the public need for a road that goes nowhere, but rather their purpose was to defend their county against encroachment by Anglos.

This case was initially argued before a Hispanic judge and was concluded, pending appeal, before an Anglo judge. The ethnic divide between plaintiffs and defendants added a dimension of difficulty that is perhaps unusual in our judicial system – yet it is becoming more common. As our nation's population continues to expand in diversity, this type of situation will be encountered with greater frequency.

<u>Sowerwine vs. Stockton (1982)</u>

As previously mentioned, Sowerwine requested a jury trial in the Complaint filed in September of 1982. We subsequently asked the judge to strike the jury demand in favor of a bench trial. We got our wish, for better or for worse.

In this case, it was not a concern about the composition of a jury that caused me to opt out of a jury trial, but rather the belief that the judge was already biased against Sowerwine and could be persuaded more easily than a panel of novices. A jury in a small Wyoming town would have been composed of individuals much like me. Almost all would have been non-Hispanic Anglos. Although individual levels of education and income would have varied, there would have been very little disparity between me and anyone on the panel. And almost all would have known Sowerwine either personally or by reputation. I had every reason to believe the panel would truly be a jury of my peers. Perhaps we outsmarted ourselves by asking for a bench trial.

Here's the moral of this story:

If you someday find yourself faced with a choice between a jury trial and a bench trial, try to determine how well you might identify with the members of a jury and how they might identify with you. If you are the party bringing suit, you have the option to choose between a jury trial and a trial before a judge. Likewise, if you are the party being sued and you oppose the plaintiff's choice, you may file a motion asking the Court to consider your position instead. A judge will make the final decision.

Neither option is without its pitfalls. If you are dealing with complicated issues that require analytical examination, you might be better off presenting your case before a judge rather than before a jury panel. The same might hold true if you don't believe you will identify well with the jurors. If you choose a jury trial, you must convince a majority of the jury panel that you are correct; the defense need only plant the seed of doubt in the minds of a few strong jurors in order to upset your entire case. However, if you opt to have your case heard before a judge, that one individual will rule thumbs up or thumbs down on your case. You must hope that the judge is honest, unbiased and intelligent and that he/she takes the time to consider your case seriously.

It is worth noting that the overwhelming majority of contract cases are heard before a judge at bench trial. The notable exception is cases pertaining to employment discrimination, most of which are argued before a jury. In either circumstance – jury trial or bench trial – plaintiffs historically win slightly more often than defendants in contract or non-contract related cases, excluding real property cases, where defendants have the historical edge.

There is no absolute litmus test to help you make this decision, but it is an important decision nonetheless. Take the time to discuss the options at length with your attorney, and give the matter your full consideration. It might be among the most important decisions you make in the prosecution or defense of your case.

<u>Misconception</u>: *The law favors those who play by the rules.*

<u>Advice</u>: *The legal system is not as sensitive to the rules as you might expect. Watch out for those who don't play by the rules.*

I have always been taught that if I played by the rules, I would eventually win out over those who resorted to trickery or cheating to attain their goals. That dictum was instilled in me by my parents and my grandparents as well as my teachers, my coaches and the parents of the other kids I grew up with. Although I knew the bad guys won occasionally, I believed the path to success and happiness was paved with honesty and hard work. I have never really questioned that.

It was therefore extremely interesting to me when my opponents in court made no attempts to hide their failures, but rather attempted to pin their failures on me.

E.O. Sowerwine and his family never denied that they had failed to deliver the repurchase monies to the designated bank by the deadline specified in the repurchase agreement. Instead, they said that it was my actions – and in some cases, inactions – that had prevented them from tendering the money on time. I suppose I should have been flattered by their implication that I held such sway in the banking community that I, at the age of 34, could wield enough influence to convince every financial institution in the State of Wyoming to deny the Sowerwines' loan requests.

Likewise, LSI never denied that they had breached the Software License Agreements or the Consulting Agreement. While they never admitted to any breach, they acknowledged they had failed to deliver the Software as per the terms to which they had agreed, and they had failed to provide us access to their Internet-based valuation system as they were obligated to do. They also acknowledged they had failed to deliver the release of the covenant not to compete on a timely basis. LSI, like the Sowerwines, claimed that they were not responsible for their failures. Unlike the Sowerwines, LSI did not attempt to lay the blame for their non-performance on us; instead they simply claimed they should not be held responsible for their failures.

Neither of these adversaries – one who sued me and the other whom we sued – denied that they had failed to meet their obligations to perform under the contracts they had executed and to which they had agreed. The validity of the contracts was never questioned. They just didn't want to be subject to the consequences of their failures. They hadn't played by the rules, but they demanded they be declared victorious. That puzzled me then and it puzzles me now.

The lesson I took from those experiences is that people often do not play by the rules, but that may have no relevance at court. If someone can successfully shift the responsibility for their actions (or inactions) from themselves to you in a court of law, they can avoid the consequences of their actions/inactions and go about their business just as though they had complied with their obligations. In today's society, that occurs more and more often. People are less willing to take responsibility for their actions, and that has contributed to the rapid increase in the number of lawsuits filed in the U.S. each year. An ever-increasing number of individuals and companies are willing and able to defend their actions in court – with a straight face – by placing blame on someone else, whether it is merited or not. Their credo seems to be "Avoid responsibility at all cost." It has become the American way.

During the many years we worked with LSI, we were never once criticized for our performance nor was the Software ever subject to criticism. We always performed on time and met or exceeded LSI's expectations with respect to our performance. The value estimates generated by our Software for the benefit of LSI were judged to be the most accurate produced by any national valuation system in independent testing by Standard & Poor.

On the other hand, LSI only performed 100% as agreed on one of the many contracts we made with them over the years. That was a lease agreement that allowed us to use their office facilities during the time we lived in Pittsburgh and helped them implement the valuation system. With that single exception, LSI failed to perform part or all of its obligations on all remaining agreements.

LSI even went so far as to put together a phony document on one occasion. In 2004, LSI's attorneys discovered (as a result of demands made by our attorney) that LSI had failed and refused to give us the release of our covenant not to compete as they were required to do in March of 2003 under the terms of the amendment to the Consulting Agreement. They quickly put one together and mailed it to our counsel with no letter of explanation. During the prior 15 months, we and our attorney had made repeated requests for the release. Suddenly in July of 2004 our attorney received a release dated April of 2003, executed by someone whose name we did not know, from a company we were unfamiliar with. We were aware that LSI had sold in early 2003 to Fidelity National Financial, but this release was executed by

Chicago Title Insurance Company. We could only assume that LSI's lawyers were trying to "create evidence" in the event our dispute over this matter ever went to court. By backdating this illegitimate release, they endeavored to imply that they had actually delivered the release in a timely fashion, in accordance with the terms of the agreement. Interestingly, when we did sue LSI in November of 2004, they never attempted to legitimize this bogus document to the court.

The point is that throughout our dealings with LSI, we played by the rules. LSI did not. That distinction had no relevance at court. LSI's alleged bad-faith conduct, evidenced by various contract breaches, was never once a topic of dispute during briefs or hearings. Instead, LSI acknowledged their shortcomings but denied any culpability.

I can't help but recall the time when I was in elementary school and accidentally tossed a baseball through a classroom window after school was out for the day. No one saw me do it. I told my parents about it that evening and they instructed me to confess to my mistake first thing the next morning and offer to pay for the window to be replaced. The cost of fixing the window would come out of my allowance until my parents had been fully reimbursed. I did as I was told, and to my surprise it wasn't a painful experience at all. It actually felt good to take responsibility for my own actions, despite the cost. I suppose I could have blamed the accident on someone or something else – or I could have been altogether silent about it. Had I chosen that path, I believe I would feel uncomfortable with my decision to this day. My guess is that LSI doesn't give me or their broken promises a moment's thought, and our system of justice does not require them to.

My advice to my children today is an elaboration on the advice I received as a child:

"Play by the rules, but also watch out for those who *don't* play by the rules."

Misconception: *Judges are infallible.*
Advice: *Like individuals in other occupations, judges can be good or bad. Judges are just people, and as such, they are subject to the same shortcomings as you and I.*

Like most people, I had always assumed that judges are individuals with extraordinary wisdom and an impeccable grasp of legal matters. Except for the occasional crook (every profession has some) I imagined judges are, for the most part, honest and hard working. I believed they care about justice. I had never really questioned the quality of judges until one of my attorneys enlightened me.

First of all, I was told, judges are not always the best and brightest attorneys. If they were, they would probably have remained in private practice making a bazillion dollars a year. They may not have graduated at the bottom of their classes, but they were probably not the cream of the crop. Surprisingly, in some jurisdictions, judges aren't required to have any legal training at all. A law degree is not even a prerequisite for our U.S. Supreme Court Justices!

Second, and perhaps of greater importance, judges are political beings. They are either appointed or elected, and in both cases they are apt to be influenced by those who appointed them or helped them get elected.

In 39 states, at least some judges are elected. In a Gallup Poll conducted in February of 2009, a whopping 89% of those surveyed (1,027 adults) thought that judges might be unduly influenced by campaign contributions – and that could lead to bias or outright corruption. There seems to be consensus that judges should remove themselves from cases where campaign support might prejudice their rulings. Although state judicial codes vary considerably, many states leave this decision entirely up to the individual judges themselves.

In his 2007 book entitled *The Nine*, which provides an insider's look at the U.S. Supreme Court, Jeffrey Toobin concludes:

"*When it comes to the core of the Court's work . . . it is ideology, not craft or skill, that controls the outcome of cases.*"

Mr. Toobin acknowledges that *political* judgment is often the overriding factor in the judicial process. In my case against LSI filed in 2004, this became an extremely poignant observation.

At the time we filed suit against LSI, they were a wholly owned subsidiary of Fidelity National Financial – in 2007, number 264 on the Fortune 500 list of the top 500 United States public corporations as measured by gross revenue. The law firm that represented them in our case was Morgan, Lewis & Bockius LLP of Philadelphia – the country's tenth largest law firm by their own estimation. Do you imagine these two companies had any political influence? Ponder this:

We filed our lawsuit against LSI on November 8, 2004. On June 8, 2005, LSI filed preliminary objections, asking the court to dismiss the case on the grounds of legal insufficiency. Their request was denied by Judge O'Reilly on August 2, 2005. On January 4, 2006, the case was scheduled for trial on May 10, 2006 by the calendar control judge, Eugene Strassburger. Shortly thereafter, LSI filed a Motion to Stay Proceedings in an attempt to get the case removed from the Court of Common Pleas in favor of non-binding mediation. That motion was denied by Judge Strassburger on February 15, 2006. On April 5th – hardly one month before the trial was to begin – LSI filed a Motion for Summary Judgment, asking the court again to dismiss the case on the basis that there was no merit to our complaint. Their motion was again denied by Judge Strassburger, who ordered the trial to proceed on May10th. At the same time, he passed control of the case to the trial judge, Judge Scanlon. Never ones to give up, LSI's counsel petitioned Judge Scanlon on May 2, 2006, asking that he grant them an immediate hearing for Summary Judgment (dismissal) or, alternatively, postpone the trial. They said they needed more time to prepare. Apparently their seven attorneys had not had adequate time during the preceding 18 months to get ready for trial. Judge Scanlon recognized the hypocrisy of their requests and denied LSI's motions. Then an odd thing happened.

Two days later, on May 4th – just days before the trial was to begin – LSI presented a motion before Judge Strassburger (the calendar control judge who had relinquished control of the case to Judge Scanlon) asking that the trial be delayed. Judge Strassburger not only granted the delay, he ordered that a Motion for Summary Judgment would be heard by Judge Scanlon on June 12th.

So, in the week before the trial was to begin, the calendar control judge who had passed control of the case to the trial judge, granted a delay of the proceeding and also ordered a hearing on summary judgment, for which there was no motion before him. Keep in mind that both the calendar control judge and the trial judge had previously denied this same motion for summary judgment within the weeks leading up to this moment, and nothing had changed in the interim. If that sounds fishy to you, I can tell you it did to me also.

We immediately filed a Motion to Vacate Judge Strassburger's decision with Judge Wettick, Strassburger's superior at the Allegheny County Court of Common Pleas. In the motion, we asked that Judge Strassburger's decision be set aside because it violated the court's rules of procedure. Judge Wettick refused to hear our request. He replied that our only recourse was to file a Motion for Reconsideration with Judge Strassburger himself.

We filed the Motion for Reconsideration, asking Judge Strassburger to re-evaluate his decision on the grounds that his order violated the "coordinate jurisdiction rule." That rule of court was created to insure that one party, disappointed with a judge's order, could not try to obtain a more favorable ruling on the identical matter from another judge. Judge Strassburger denied our motion. We were at a dead end. Having failed to get the court order overturned, we began to prepare for the Hearing on Motion for Summary Judgment scheduled for June 12th.

A judge does have the authority to dismiss a case before trial if there appears to be insufficient grounds for the prosecution of the case. Although Judge Scanlon had presumably reviewed our complaint (it being only days before the established trial date), at the Hearing on Motion for Summary Judgment we submitted a new brief to Judge Scanlon pointing out all the reasons why our case should be heard. We advised that there were several issues of fact that needed to be resolved, and stated that the only proper forum for argument was at trial in the Court of Common Pleas where evidence could be proffered and testimony could be heard. LSI filed their brief in favor of immediate dismissal. The oral presentation held on June 12th was a brief affair. On June 27th, we were advised that Judge Scanlon had granted LSI's Motion for Summary Judgment. No opinion or memorandum of explanation accompanied the order, so we had no way of knowing why Scanlon had ruled the way he did. The order simply stated that LSI's Motion for Summary Judgment had been granted, and we were out of court. Just like that. After one year and ten months of preparation, we were told there would be no trial.

I found it interesting – and frustrating – that a judge could rule one day that our case had enough substance to merit a full hearing at trial, and only days later issue a ruling that contradicted that previous conclusion when there had been no change in the evidence before him.

So much for the adage that we are all entitled to our day in court.

It might be unfair to presume that there was some political hanky-panky behind all of this. We will never know for certain. We did call this out-of-the-ordinary procedure into question when we appealed the case to the Superior Court of Pennsylvania. At that time we asserted that Judge Strassburger's actions had violated the coordinate jurisdiction rule in the Commonwealth of Pennsylvania that prohibits "shopping" for a judge who is willing to give a specific ruling on a particular issue. The rule says if you don't get the decision you're looking for, you can't go to another judge in the same district and get a different, more favorable, ruling from him. That's precisely what occurred, but we never could get any court in Pennsylvania to acknowledge that Judge Strassburger's actions had been sufficiently out of line to overturn his order and allow us to continue to trial.

One additional comment: Judges are immune to prosecution for errors of judgment – even if those errors were committed intentionally. There's not much you can do to defend yourself against that, and if it happens to you, you have no recourse. I'll bet that's one you hadn't thought of.

Was our experience with the court system in Pennsylvania influenced by local politics? Perhaps. We'll never know. But then we're not big contributors.

<u>*Misconception*</u>: *Facts are facts.*
<u>*Advice*</u>: *Facts are only facts if the court acknowledges them as facts.*

There are two essential components to every argument at court; the argument must be based both in fact and in law. Whereas an argument supported by legal precedent might carry the day, one that is based solely on factual evidence might be inadequate to secure a sought-after decision. Let me give you an example.

In our case with LSI, the Defendants raised several reasons why we should be barred from suing them over their repeated failures to perform under the terms of the Software License Agreements, as amended. Among the defenses they raised was the assertion that our litigation should be disallowed because we were claiming "lost profits," since we had been denied the use of the Software that LSI was to have delivered to us. LSI declared we could not sue for lost profits because the original Software License Agreements contained clauses barring us from doing so.

Here is the Limitation on Liability clause that appeared in each of the Software License Agreements:

"LIMITATION ON LIABILITY. NEITHER LSI NOR ITS PARENT OR ANY OF LSI'S AFFILIATES WILL BE LIABLE TO ESI FOR ANY DIRECT, SPECIAL, INCIDENTAL, CONSEQUENTIAL, INDIRECT OR PUNITIVE DAMAGES ARISING FROM OR RELATING TO ESI's USE OF THE SOFTWARE AND DOCUMENTATION EVEN IF LSI HAS BEEN ADVISED OF THE POSSIBILITY OF SUCH DAMAGES. NEITHER LSI NOR ANY OF ITS AFFILIATES WILL BE RESPONSIBLE FOR LOST PROFITS OR REVENUES, LOSS OF USE OF THE SOFTWARE, LOSS OF DATA, COSTS OF RE-CREATING LOST DATA, COMPUTER VIRUSES, COMMUNICATION LINE FAILURE, THE COST OF ANY SUBSTITUTE EQUIPMENT OR PROGRAM, OTHER PECUNIARY LOSS OR CLAIMS BY ANY PARTY. LSI's entire liability and ESI's sole and exclusive remedy as to the Software will be to terminate the Agreement by destroying all copies of the Software."

As a software developer, I have been party to dozens of these Limitation on Liability clauses over the years. I have authored a number of them myself. I know what they mean and I know what they are intended to avoid. The provision prevents a user of the Software (us) from suing the provider of the Software (LSI) in the event the Software doesn't work as intended and the user incurs some monetary loss as a result. The provision is almost always accompanied by a

Disclaimer of Warranties that specifies the user (us) is aware that the Software is being provided on an "as is" basis, and no warrants or representations are made as to the soundness of the Software. Just such a clause did indeed precede the Limitation on Liability provision in the Software License Agreements.

You might ask why anyone who is buying software would agree to such a provision. I can't answer that, except to say it is standard phraseology in many software licensing and software sale agreements. I can say that the provision didn't alarm us – we had written the Software and knew precisely what we were getting. We had used the Software in a commercial setting for years and knew it to be exactly what we wanted. No warrants or representations were necessary.

In their defense, LSI argued that the only valid interpretation of the Limitation on Liability clause was straightforward – we could not sue for lost profits. We replied that LSI's interpretation was not only incorrect, but misleading. We asserted that the provision barred us from suing LSI for any "*DAMAGES ARISING FROM OR RELATING TO ESI's USE OF THE SOFTWARE AND DOCUMENTATION....*" Since LSI had never delivered the Software to us as they were obligated to do, we were not asking for damages related to the *use* of the Software, but rather from LSI's failure and refusal to *give* us the Software. LSI contended that the provision barred us from suing for lost profits – period. We had a disagreement that, in my opinion, any judge applying common sense could sort out. That wasn't good enough.

Our attorney suggested we counter the defense with a legal strategy in addition to a common sense discussion of the intent of the provision. He pointed out that according to LSI's narrow interpretation of the Limitation on Liability terms we had but a single remedy provided by the clause – we could destroy the Software as the last line of the provision indicated. Since we had never received the Software, we obviously could not destroy it. Hence, according to LSI's explanation, we had no remedy. In law, a provision that provides no remedy is invalid and unenforceable.

The argument made perfect sense to us, so our counsel began the search for case law that would support our argument. He searched and he searched, but could find no case that had ever been tried in the State of Pennsylvania where a Limitation on Liability clause had been used to bar litigation in the exact same manner. He did, however, find a case that had been argued before the Superior Court of Pennsylvania that dealt with the issue of Limitation on Liability, albeit in a different context.

In that case, a Defendant claimed that the Plaintiff could not sue him because a Limitation on Liability clause prevented him from doing so. The Court agreed. In its decision, the Court stated that since the Limitation on Liability provision *afforded the Plaintiff a remedy*, the Plaintiff had to accept that remedy rather than pursue litigation. That was what the parties had agreed to. The Court further stated that the decision was intentionally silent as to what their opinion might have been had there been *no* remedy.

Since our case had been thrown out of Court by Judge Scanlon in 2006 when he granted LSI a Motion on Summary Judgment, our first opportunity to argue our position came at the time of our appeal to the Pennsylvania Superior Court. At our hearing in June of 2007 we discovered that one of the judges on our panel – Judge Tamilia – had participated in the ruling just described.

Recognizing that the Court had not dealt with the issue of Limitation on Liability where *no* remedy was available, and recognizing that Judge Tamilia was party to that decision, we asked during our hearing that the Court address the matter head on. We explained our position, referenced the prior court decision, and requested that the Court now address the particular circumstance they had avoided in the earlier opinion.

Unfortunately, the Court chose to ignore our request and ignored the issue altogether. They failed to make any mention of the issue of Limitation on Liability in their October 1, 2007 opinion, and denied our request that the case be remanded back to the Court of Common Pleas for trial, on the basis of other issues. By ignoring this particular issue they also ignored a matter of significant fact that might have influenced the outcome of the case if it had been properly addressed by the Court.

In this case neither common sense nor point of law moved the judges to give us a favorable ruling on a salient issue. We appealed the Superior Court's decision to the Pennsylvania Supreme Court, but that court also chose to ignore this issue altogether.

Regardless of my experience, a well-constructed argument at court should include both of the components described: a common sense explanation of how the facts fit applicable law, and case law that supports the circumstances as they appear in the Complaint. If both elements are present, and if they are communicated clearly and succinctly, there is greater probability that you will receive a favorable decision.

Misconception: *The law is the law.*
Advice: *The law as interpreted by one judge might have very different implications than the same law as interpreted by another judge.*

There is an inclination to believe that the law is the law; there is no deviation in the law. This isn't correct on any number of levels, but specifically because the laws of the land are open to so much interpretation and re-evaluation by the judiciary.

Evaluation Services, Inc. vs. Lender's Service, Inc. (2006)

In our second case against LSI, we accused LSI of a breach of our Consulting Agreement as amended on August 1, 2002. Under the terms of the agreement, LSI promised to release us from our covenant not to compete in the automated valuation industry as long as we performed certain tasks within a specified time period. We performed, and they failed and refused to deliver the release.

The 2002 amendment stipulated that any dispute arising out of the agreement be arbitrated rather than litigated. Consequently, we filed a demand for arbitration in September of 2006. LSI asserted that we should be barred from arbitration because they said we had made the claim for breach of the Consulting Agreement in our case filed with the Court of Common Pleas in 2004. They asserted that we should not be allowed to bring up the identical issue in another venue in order to obtain a different opinion. We denied their allegation, saying we had never made this claim at Court, and soon found ourselves back in front of a judge trying to protect our right to seek damages for LSI's breach.

At issue was a section of Count IV of our original suit filed in 2004, which Count was entitled:

Breach of Implied Covenant of Good Faith and Fair Dealing

The second paragraph of Count IV read, in part:

By virtue of the parties' Software Purchase Agreement, the amendments thereto, the Software License Agreements and amendments thereto, as well as the Agreements executed November 12, 2002, there arose a duty on the part of LSI to act in good faith and with fair dealing with regard to its performance of its obligations in favor of Willman and ESI. Your Plaintiffs aver that LSI has engaged in bad-faith conduct throughout the course of the respective parties' contractual obligations and course of dealing in the following respects:

a. *In failing to provide the valuation software and internet access in violation of the Willman Software License Agreement and amendment thereto;*

b. *In failing to provide the valuation software and internet access in violation of the ESI Software Licensing Agreement and amendments thereto;*

c. *In failing to waive, in a timely manner, the covenants against competition contained in the Software Purchase Agreement dated September 30, 1997, as provided for in the Second Amendment to Consulting Agreement executed on November 12, 2002.*

d. *In failing to provide the personnel and resources required under the November 12, 2002, Agreement;*

e. *In its breach of the terms and spirit of the Software Purchase Agreement and the subsequent amendments thereto;*

f. *In fraudulently misrepresenting its intentions with regard to its explicit promises made under the*

> *Agreement executed November 12, 2002, as well as its failure to disclose the negotiations with Fidelity*

all of which constitute a breach of the implied covenant of good faith and fair dealing with regard to the parties' contracts, course of dealing, and exclusivity relationship with regard to the subject software.

Before I go further, let me refer you to Rule 1020 of the Pennsylvania Legal Code, which states:

(a) The plaintiff may state in the complaint more than one cause of action cognizable in a civil action against the same defendant. Each cause of action and any special damage related thereto shall be stated in a separate count containing a demand for relief.

Our original Complaint contained five Counts (i.e. causes of action or claims). Each was stated separately, as required by Rule 1020, and each contained a demand for relief. Within our Count IV, we cited several examples of LSI's bad faith conduct – among them, LSI's failure to release us from our agreement not to compete, as required by the terms of the 2002 amendment to the Consulting Agreement (item c above). The important distinction here is that we cited several *examples* of LSI's bad faith conduct; we did not make several *claims* regarding their conduct. We made only one claim (Count) – LSI had acted in bad faith.

The examples cited in Count IV did not meet the definition of "cause of action" (claim) set forth in Rule 1020, nor were they intended to. The claim in Count IV was for Breach of the Implied Covenant of Good Faith and Fair Dealing. Other Counts dealt with other claims – one claim per Count, each containing a demand for relief. In fact, examples *a* and *b* listed in Count IV were set forth as separate and distinct Counts (I and II), and it was those Counts we ultimately decided to litigate. Had we decided to bring claims against LSI for any of the other issues cited as examples, we would have been required to articulate those claims in separate and distinct Counts as well. We might have done so with regard to LSI's failure to release us from our agreement not to compete had we not been barred from doing so by the terms of the Amendment to the Consulting Agreement that specified disputes had to be arbitrated rather than litigated.

On January 24, 2007, LSI filed a Motion for Summary Judgment with the Court of Common Pleas, requesting that the case be summarily dismissed. A hearing on LSI's motion was held on April 9th at the Allegheny County Courthouse before Judge Judith Friedman. Regardless of the straightforward nature of the distinction between a claim and a comment made in support of a claim, Judge Friedman agreed with LSI and granted the dismissal. In her decision, she stated that we had made a claim in Court—in our Count IV—regarding LSI's breach of the amendment to the Consulting Agreement, even though we had never prosecuted that claim. She therefore ruled we were forever barred from taking that claim before any court or any arbitration panel ever again.

Once again, we appealed the decision to the Superior Court of Pennsylvania.

We obviously disagreed with the Judge Friedman's decision in this case. Was our disagreement based on a difference in our interpretations of the rule of law and the circumstances of our case? Apparently. In her defense of her ruling, Judge Friedman was absolutely insulting. She raged that hers was a reasoned decision founded in fact, and she expressed total disregard for our "uninformed" assertions.

There you have it. The law apparently is not the law.

PREPARE YOURSELF FOR THE LEGAL PROCESS

If you have read this far, you probably have some sense that the legal process is a road with more hazards than you might have imagined. In order to enter the fray and come out whole, you need to prepare for the financial, emotional ride you are about to take. The process takes a degree of time, money and emotional stability that probably surpasses your initial expectations.

Time

The litigation process takes time, and there are many reasons that it does. First of all, when one party files a Complaint against another, the Defendant (the one being sued) needs time to respond to the claim. The Defendant has to be given adequate time to respond, and will often request additional time – which is nearly always granted as long as the request is reasonable. In response to the Complaint, the Defendant might possibly make a counterclaim against the Plaintiff (the one who filed the original claim). If that's the case, the Plaintiff needs time to respond. Often, a Defendant will assert that the claim being brought is frivolous and has no legal basis, and will file a motion asking the court to dismiss the suit in its entirety (such as a Motion for Summary Judgment). The Plaintiff must be afforded time to respond to that motion, and so it goes. Sometimes this form of bickering by filing motions seems to go on forever. Every filing adds weeks to the process.

At some point, the parties enter the "discovery phase" of the process, meaning they begin to accumulate facts pertaining to the case from their opponents. Each party will send the other a list of questions to be answered within a limited time period, and returned (interrogatories). The parties will also probably ask each other to provide documents and correspondence that might help explain the facts (request for documents). In addition, they may want to ask questions of key persons, under oath, to discern the facts or identify weaknesses in the opponent's case (depositions). Depending on the availability of the people to be questioned, the discovery period can add weeks or months to the process.

When it becomes evident that the parties are not going to settle their differences outside of court and they have supplied the court with the requisite filings, a trial date will be set. Subject to the case load of the available judges, the trial date might be several months in the future. Depending upon the circumstances, it can take substantially longer to get to trial (shortage of judges, time of year, etc.).

Prior to the trial date, a pre-trial hearing is usually held. Here, the judge often tries to enlighten the parties as to the prudence of settling their dispute without going to trial. If unsuccessful, the hearing becomes a forum to make certain everything and every party is ready for trial.

If nothing has happened to cause the process to jump the track (no more hearings or unusual motions that need to be dealt with), the trial is held. Whether it is a jury trial or a trial before a judge alone, the time allocated to the trial is about the same, and depends on the complexity of the case, the number of witnesses the parties intend to call and the number of exhibits they intent to submit. Trial could take a day, several days, or weeks.

It would be nice to think the process ends with the trial. It generally does not. If the trial is a jury trial, a verdict will be rendered after all evidence has been submitted and arguments have been made. If the trial is a bench trial, the judge has the option of ruling from the bench – rendering a decision at the end of the trial – but that seldom happens. More often the judge will take the case "under advisement," and the decision might be months in coming. In our lawsuit with Rio Arriba County over the disposition of our ranch road, the judge did not rule until eleven months after the trial.

Start to finish, it is not unusual for the process to consume one to two years. This seems terribly unfair if you're the one who feels he/she has been wronged and is seeking some sort of restitution. The judiciary comes across as being insensitive and callous, when in reality their caseload may simply be more than they can possibly be expected to handle efficiently. Regardless, it's frustrating to the parties involved – especially if they are individuals rather than corporations – and the duration of the process adds to the cost.

Appeal anyone? Add another year or two.

I must add that as I have personally traveled this path through several of our nation's courts, I have been astonished time and again at the patience displayed by attorneys sitting in the courtroom. On the days when hearings are scheduled and individual attorneys are required to be in attendance at court, they can be obligated to sit for hours waiting to make their presentations. All the while, they are forced to listen to some of the most outrageous presentations imaginable, by their fellow lawyers. I must tell you, I have been very unimpressed with the cognitive skills of lawyers at large. Few seem capable of organizing their thoughts and articulating a well constructed argument. That must drive judges crazy. It certainly drives a lot of Plaintiffs and Defendants wild, for they are often advised to attend these hearings as well.

One consequence of this is that hearings can take longer than they might otherwise, and it becomes virtually impossible to predict when any particular case might be heard. That leads to a great deal of wasted time for all concerned. It is the attorneys in the audience, awaiting their turns at the podium, who appear to sit most patiently. Perhaps that is because they have learned that others might have reason to be impatient with them, on occasion.

<u>Cost</u>

The cost of litigation can vary depending on the approach you take and whether there is someone to share the cost with you. The two primary options you might have available to you are:

a) to pay the costs personally, or

b) to share the costs with your attorney on a contingency basis

This second option may not be available to you depending on the attorney you have hired and the circumstances of the case. If it is a possibility, you might be able to convince your attorney's firm to participate in the cost of litigation by allowing them to participate in any reward that might be derived as a result of the litigation. Quite often, the law firm's take is disproportionate to the amount of their risk (larger), but if you ask them to share in the risk you can expect that. If your resources are not adequate to fight the fight, this might be your only alternative.

Not all firms will take cases on a contingency basis, and not all firms that will are willing to take all cases on that basis. Law firms have expenses and cash flow needs just like individuals do, and not all firms are financially able to forgo fee income with the expectation of splitting the pie if the case is successfully litigated. If the firm you select has the financial capacity to entertain such a possible partnership – for that's what the venture becomes, in essence – you can bet they will be very selective with regard to the number and type of cases they accept on a contingency basis. Bottom line – law firms are in business to make money, not to take unnecessary risks.

And they do make money. The fees associated with a court case add up quickly, especially at the beginning when the finale seems (and is) a long way off. First are the attorney fees. A good lawyer will cost several hundred dollars an hour, as of this writing. He or she will generally be supported by associates whose time is billed at a lesser amount, and who will help with the necessary research and leg work. Don't be fooled into thinking that the associate will handle the lion's share of the work because that might not be the case. There will be times when your attorney and one or two associates will be working on your case concurrently, and your hourly costs will accrue at an astronomical pace. However, if you want good representation you must be prepared to pay the piper (or the lawyer, in this instance).

Attorney fees are only part of the costs associated with a court case. There are endless filing fees, fees for copying documents, fees for delivering and/or mailing documents, fees for court reporters, fees to cover every expense your attorney incurs in conjunction with your case. Before you hire your attorney, it's advisable to have a little talk about this aspect of the cost. We all know it's much easier to spend someone else's money than it is our own. We are much more diligent watching our own pennies – less so with others'. Ask your attorney to be sensitive to this.

There is no average cost for a lawsuit. They are all expensive. We always hear that the only one who wins in a lawsuit is the lawyer, and that is quite often the reality. The parties to a suit don't know whether they will win or lose; presumably they both believe they will win. The lawyers always know they will win as long as their clients continue to pay their monthly invoices on time. Your attorney should be able to give you a reasonable cost estimate before you become engaged in the process, and you need to ask. You probably won't get a guaranteed estimate because unforeseen things can happen in any case; your opponent can cause you to respond to motions and attend hearings that were not anticipated – just to try to starve you out. This is standard operating procedure. Since you can't count on your winnings to pay the bills any more than you could if you were entering a crap game, you must have access to a war chest that is adequate to see you through from start to finish. That could be a few thousand dollars or it could be tens of thousands of dollars – even hundreds of thousands. Try to get a reasonable estimate of costs up front, and then prepare to spend – as we have already seen – for a long time.

During my personal career as a participant in litigation – and it *does* feel like it's been a career sometimes – I and those on my side of the case have incurred costs in excess of three quarters of a million dollars. Luckily, I have not had to foot the entire bill by myself. My attorneys in the Sowerwine case assumed part of the cost, albeit unintentionally. I lost so much money in that case that I couldn't pay my final bill. My partner shared some of the expenses in the initial case against LSI, and in the Velasquez case our title company intervened. Thank heavens we and our neighbors purchased extended title coverage that provided protection against matters that were not of record. That saved us hundreds of thousands of dollars.

Emotional Cost

Even if you have approached pending litigation with a good degree of common sense and feel you have asked all the right questions – interviewed attorneys, anticipated costs, planned for a reasonable amount of time to get though the process – I assure you that you will encounter a good many surprises along the way. It is perhaps the uncertainty associated with litigation that is the most difficult aspect to deal with. You find yourself second guessing the opposition, your attorney, the judge and even your own instincts. You find yourself on an emotional roller coaster ride unlike anything you have experienced before, and it's no thrill. It's uncomfortable.

I am a person who handles stress quite well, yet soon after being sued by the Sowerwines in 1982 I experienced a heart arrhythmia – an irregular heartbeat – that landed me in the intensive care ward of the local hospital. The precise cause was never determined, but the timing of the episode seems more than coincidental. The doctors eventually decided the event was stress-related. I recovered with no lasting side effects, but during subsequent litigation I have occasionally felt the need to separate myself from what is happening by taking a walk or exercising in order to control my breathing and the pace of my heart. If you are a person who handles day-to-day stress well, you might be surprised by how mentally and physically taxing the stress of litigation can be.

You won't be the only one feeling the stress of the litigation. If you are married or in a meaningful relationship that you value, be prepared to spend a lot of effort protecting that relationship. I don't know whether men or women are better equipped for the emotional ups and downs of a court case and the impact of those twists and turns on private life. The opposing attorney in my suit with Sowerwine commented during my deposition that I seemed to be taking the entire matter too personally. I asked what he expected. It is impossible *not* to take it personally, in my opinion. It *is* personal. In litigation, you are either seeking to recover something that has been denied you (or that someone is trying to take from you), or you are defending your actions against the allegations of an accuser. In either case, you are dealing with an adversary who will often say or do whatever is necessary to prevail against you. You are in a brawl that can be as emotionally charged as a prize fight. It might be the most personal thing you are ever involved in outside of your relationship with a loved one, and it is not a pleasant experience.

I don't believe you can adequately prepare for the emotional ride, because it is so unpredictable. Suffice it to say that you must plan to spend many evenings discussing the progress of the case with your partner. Be open to all discussion, be honest about your thoughts and be sensitive to your partner's feelings. Depending on the circumstances of your case, you might think you're the one going through the ordeal – but you're not the only one. Your case impacts your family directly, and although you might not want or need that added pressure at the time, you've got it. Don't ignore it. You might even decide to walk away from the case if the battle jeopardizes a cherished relationship.

There is no question that the strain of the lawsuit with Sowerwine in the early 1980s contributed to the breakup of my first marriage. It takes a very strong marriage indeed to withstand the emotional and financial strains imposed by years of litigation. By 2004, when we decided to sue LSI, I was remarried, and my wife and I discussed the practicality of suing a large company and the probability that we could succeed. I won't say we entered the litigation with our eyes wide open, but we were much better prepared than I had been years earlier – primarily because of my prior experience in the Sowerwine case. Even though my present wife and I were better equipped to handle the ups and downs of the suit with LSI, we were both dropped to our knees when we received a call from our attorney at the end of June, 2006 telling us he had bad news. Judge Scanlon had ruled against us in the hearing on LSI's Motion for Summary Judgment, and we were essentially out of court. To add insult to injury, LSI asked the court to make us pay their lawyer fees and court costs (which the court eventually denied). Nothing could have prepared us for that ruling, and in the weeks that followed we had many frank discussions about whether we should file an appeal and keep the case going.

We did file the appeal and during the preparation of the appeal brief, when we really dug deeply into Judge Scanlon's decision, my wife and I both became incensed at what we construed to be his disregard for the facts of the case and his misapplication of law. Interestingly, this terribly distressing time actually steeled our mutual resolve and brought us closer together. Despite the setbacks we faced as we continued our battle, my wife and I have never doubted our decision to fight on, and we have never doubted one another.

There was one casualty during our lawsuit with LSI, and that was my partner. He first began to voice reservations when LSI countersued us in March of 2006. In an outrageous maneuver to scare us off, LSI claimed that if the court found the Settlement & Release Agreement to be invalid – the agreement for which LSI had failed to deliver full consideration – we should be forced to return the amount of any royalties we had received subsequent to that Agreement or we would be "unjustly enriched." This tactic is not uncommon – the attempt to defuse a suit by filing a countersuit. We took it seriously, but I failed to see how any judge could be swayed to agree with the convoluted reasoning set forth in the countersuit. The filing hardly gave me pause, but it did concern my partner and, to some degree, my wife.

Finally, following Scanlon's unfathomable ruling in the matter of LSI's Motion for Summary Judgment in June of 2006, my partner said he'd had enough. He was having trouble sleeping and his stomach was upset all the time – this from a person who *always* chews his food the recommended 25 to 50 times per mouthful. The litigation process was consuming him and he decided he didn't want to proceed. We were able to work out an arrangement whereby I would continue on behalf of both of us, and he agreed to step back into the picture if and when it became necessary for him to testify or otherwise contribute. It was an agreement that satisfied both parties, but I couldn't help wondering how things might have turned out if my wife and not my partner had voiced such strong feelings.

<u>The Stigma</u>

My first experience with litigation was the Sowerwine case that began in 1982. At the moment I made the decision to defend myself against his claim, I knew I was on solid ground. His contention that I had impaired his ability to raise the money to repurchase the ranch was ludicrous. He knew it and I knew it. However, looking back from a more mature vantage point today, I view my challenge to my lawyer – "Bring him on!" – as the uninformed bravado of an inexperienced young man. While I most certainly was on solid ground (despite the outcome), my approach to the possibility of litigation was arrogant.

I was unaware of the effect this arrogance would have on my relationships with others. It took me some time to understand that when you're involved in litigation – whether you're the one suing or the one being sued – there is a stigma that attaches to you. And you don't even know it.

After making the decision not to back down from the Sowerwine suit, I showed no reluctance to tout my valor at protecting my principles whether at a cocktail party with people I knew or at a meeting with people with whom I was only slightly acquainted. I was so wrapped up in my own events that I didn't notice some people were actually beginning to see me in a different light. They might have said, "Good for you. It's refreshing to see someone stick up for his rights." However, what many really meant was "I think you're foolish, but go ahead" or "Your conviction is admirable, but I don't necessarily agree that you're right."

The fact is that people view you differently if you're involved in a lawsuit. A stigma becomes associated with you, and it is in no way admirable. There is nothing you can do to avoid it; it will happen. You must be aware of it and adjust your sensitivity to it.

A friend whom I have known for years and who knows about my ordeals at court once remarked, "I don't ever want to get into a fight with Stockton." Thinking about that comment later, I wondered what he had meant. Was he making an observation about my business acumen, or implying he didn't want to get into a fight with me because I might take him to court? The truth is that the comment had been harmless. It was my own sensitivity about being involved in litigation that led me to question the true meaning of the statement.

During the course of my business, in the years I was engaged in litigation, I found I was often asked to explain my involvement. There was no attempt to disguise the reason for the question – people needed to know if I was a "live wire" who might sue them over the slightest disagreement. My explanations were honest, but even to me they sounded feeble. I was defensive when there was no need to be defensive. The reality is that it is very hard to explain to someone why you're involved in a lawsuit without feeling guilty that you are involved. It doesn't make any difference whether you are 100% correct in your convictions and the actions that culminated in the suit were perfectly honorable. You will have trouble explaining it and people will question your character. I have no doubt my involvement in litigation has resulted in loss of business opportunities.

This book aside, I have learned to share the details of any litigation I am involved in only on a "need to know" basis.

Other Personal Costs

There are a couple of additional aspects to the process that most people don't anticipate. The first is having someone else speak on their behalf. For me, that was a trying experience. In three of the cases I have been involved in (LSI and Sowerwine) I was the individual who had the greatest knowledge of events and facts. I was able to provide input into all the briefs written by my attorneys, but the documents were ultimately their documents, and they had the final say as to structure and content. I was able to speak at my own deposition, and in one case as a witness at trial, but I found myself constantly wanting to add clarification that would reinforce friendly testimony or contradict deceptive comments by unfriendly witnesses. I'm a control freak, and as a party to a lawsuit, you are definitely not in control. I found that to be extremely frustrating.

The second aspect I found more difficult than I first imagined, was having someone for whom I had no respect question my character and integrity. When you're being questioned by opposing counsel, whether at deposition or on the witness stand, you have to field some questions that are deliberately designed to anger you or make you appear to be a person of doubtful character. The appropriate response is to take a deep breath and answer in such a manner as to set the record straight in gentlemanly fashion. That's easier said than done. Well-trained attorneys will constantly seek out your Achilles heel – the line of questioning that will cause you to shoot back a flip response that will cast doubt on your credibility and bring your facts into question. They know you are nervous and that being questioned under oath is an uncomfortable experience at best, even for the most honest of individuals. A seasoned interrogator will alternately try to confuse you and upset you with a well-chosen set of questions, and it is extremely difficult to keep your eye on the ball – to follow the questions and give accurate, appropriate answers. It's much harder than it looks when you see an actor in a movie do it.

Keep your cool. Don't allow anyone to control you or confuse you. If you don't understand a question, ask for clarification. Take the necessary time to formulate your responses before you speak. You don't have to hurry. Above all, you want your responses to be honest, accurate and complete.

PICK YOUR FIGHTS CAREFULLY

If you feel prepared for the test of litigation and choose to enter the realm of courts and lawyers and judges, pause once more before you hire an attorney and head for the courthouse. I suggest you pick your fights very carefully. Not all fights should be fought, even if you believe you're absolutely right.

When we filed suit against LSI in 2004, we listed five separate Counts in our Complaint:

Count I	Breach of Software License Agreement – LSI & Willman & Associates, Inc. (my partner's appraisal company)
Count II	Breach of Software License Agreement – LSI & Evaluation Services, Inc.
Count III	Breach of the Doctrine of Necessary Implication
Count IV	Breach of the Implied Covenant of Good Faith and Fair Dealing
Count V	Promissory Estoppel

The first two Counts dealt with relatively straightforward breach of contract issues. The remaining Counts were more obscure, dealing with matters of conduct and obligation. At the pre-trial hearing held in April of 2006, we decided to drop all but Counts I & II. We didn't drop Counts III through V because we were on shaky ground; rather, we eliminated them from our Complaint because we thought we might have difficulty proving LSI's *intent* with regard to those Counts. We didn't want to jeopardize the entire case by including Counts that might deflect the court's attention, while being difficult to prove.

Counts I & II pertained to breaches of the Software License Agreements between Willman & Associates, Inc. and LSI and also Evaluation Services, Inc. and LSI. In both of those Agreements, LSI had promised to deliver Software and to provide access to their Internet-based valuation system so the parties (we) could continue their existing valuation business in the State of Colorado. LSI failed in both respects. They breached the contracts. It mattered not *why* LSI breached the contracts, only that the breaches were committed.

On the other hand, Counts III, IV & V required us to establish the fact that LSI *intended* to commit various breaches. In those Counts, we asserted that LSI had made contractual promises they never intended to fulfill. Specifically, we claimed that at the time LSI was pleading with us not to sue them and promising to be more diligent in their management of the automated valuation system to insure increased royalty revenues to us, they were in the final stages of negotiation with Fidelity National Financial for the purchase of LSI. In fact, the sale to Fidelity was announced about 60 days after we executed our final round of agreements and amendments with LSI in November of 2002. In fact, LSI failed to perform almost everything they promised to do in those agreements. With regard to some of their obligations under certain agreements, they never even attempted to comply. We knew very well that LSI had deliberately deceived us, but could we prove it in court?

Proving *what* happened in a course of events is not terribly difficult if there is enough written documentation, first hand testimony or other irrefutable evidence to support an allegation. However, proving *why* someone acted as they did can be extremely difficult. Whereas a breach of contract for failure to perform is almost self-evident, proving that someone intended to breach a contract is tough.

We could have forged ahead with Counts III, IV and V, but we would have had to prove that LSI had deliberately and knowingly set out to deceive us – that they had never intended to perform on their obligations. Their attorneys could have responded that they were simply incompetent. Without an LSI insider willing to testify that LSI had deliberately defrauded us, it would have been next to impossible to prove our allegations. We didn't have a witness willing to blow the whistle on LSI. How do you fight that kind of fight?

We ultimately decided that our evidence, while compelling, was circumstantial; we could not prove what the management of LSI was thinking when they pushed the November 2002 agreements in front of us for our signatures, regardless of how obvious their deceit appeared in retrospect.

We had a good opportunity to recover damages for LSI's breach of the License Agreements, and we decided not to impair that prospect by adding layers of innuendo bringing the other Counts to court. We decided which fights were worth picking and which were not. In doing so, we forfeited the opportunity to sue for additional damages for matters about which we knew we had been wronged. In our opinions, we took the correct course. Could we have prevailed if we had pressed the other Counts? We'll never know. We picked our fights and walked away from those we felt were not worth pursuing.

This is an appropriate place to mention one other concern that requires consideration prior to any litigation if you are the individual making claims against another, and those claims are for monetary damages. Before filing, you must determine whether the defendant has the ability to pay the damages you are demanding, if you should win the suit. It won't do any good to spend the time and money to secure an award that can never be realized. That would definitely *not* be a fight worth picking.

SELECTING AN ATTORNEY

One of the most important decisions you will make once you become involved in a lawsuit, is the selection of the attorney you choose to represent you. It might be *the* most important decision.

You don't have to have an attorney. The law provides that you may choose to handle your own case, whether it is your defense or the prosecution of another party. I strongly advise against this. Most of us simply do not have the legal expertise to manage our own case without bungling it miserably. I have watched individuals attempt it, and the judge usually becomes so aggravated with their need for proper instruction – which adds a good deal of time to the judge's already full court schedule – that the individual alienates the judge right off the bat. That's not a good thing. While you don't have to pander to the judge, you certainly don't want him or her for an enemy.

The whole litigation process is quite structured, and the court will expect you to adhere to that structure. There are filings that must be made by certain dates, responses that are required within specified timeframes, and an entire courtroom etiquette that is choreographed like a dance. Managing the process is not something to be attempted by the uninitiated.

There is an old and apt saying: "The person who represents himself at court has a fool for an attorney." If you have a fight worth fighting, get a lawyer.

Be mindful of the fact that when you hire a lawyer you are really hiring a law firm, in most cases. Most attorneys who handle civil law cases work in offices with other attorneys and a support staff capable of handling the more mundane matters such as researching case law, and compiling and delivering court documents. Without the support of other experienced attorneys and well-trained staff, your lawyer might be ill-equipped to serve you.

Having said that, the hourly cost of an experienced attorney who practices as part of a well-run law firm can be substantial. You need to face the cost issue right up front. Are you willing (and able) to pay what is necessary to have good representation, or are you going to try to get by with less than adequate counsel? You don't have to hire the best lawyer from the biggest law firm – I'm not advocating that. However, I do suggest you seek experienced counsel with a good reputation who is part of a reputable firm.

When you interview the attorney who you think you might hire – and do take the time to interview him or her – be open and honest. Attorneys are not going to look at you like a three-headed beast because you've been sued or want to sue someone. That's what they do; they understand. You don't have to feel embarrassed.

Here are some questions you'll want to resolve when you are interviewing an attorney:

- Ask about their familiarity with the type of issue(s) you face.
- Ask about their track record. How successful have they been?

- Determine whether or not they are believable. If an attorney lacks credibility in your eyes, a jury or a judge will likely respond the same.
- Make sure the price fits your pocketbook.

I would also ask for references, but don't be put off if your request is denied. It can be difficult for an attorney to give out references because so much of what goes on between an attorney and a client is confidential. A superior approach might be to ask someone you know and respect – someone who has had occasion to hire counsel for litigation purposes – for the name of a reputable attorney. Their recommendation might yield better results.

Once you have selected your attorney, make sure you tell that individual everything you know about the case. Disclose everything; hide nothing. You must keep in mind that you are the person who is in the best position to know all the facts and circumstances surrounding your case. If you don't tell your attorney, you restrict his/her ability to provide you the best possible representation. Don't deal in half truths and don't think you can hide a little secret, hoping it will never come up at trial. It quite possibly will, and when it does it might be devastating to your case. It can also destroy the relationship between you and your attorney, and that is a relationship you need to protect. That individual will be standing in your stead throughout the litigation. If you don't have a good relationship – i.e. if your lawyer doesn't trust you (and vice versa) – your chances of coming out on top diminish greatly.

We were represented by counsel from Colorado when we negotiated the original agreements with Merrill Lynch and LSI in 1997, and we used the same attorney throughout our dealings with LSI in the years that followed. We were well satisfied with the representation and advice we had received, and when it came time to file suit against LSI, we asked that same lawyer to represent us. He informed us that he wasn't licensed in the State of Pennsylvania where the filing had to be made, but that he would help us find competent counsel. We asked if we could retain him to assist in the development of the case, and to our surprise, he said "No." We were mystified by his answer until he explained that he was so incensed by the manner in which LSI had conducted its affairs during the course of our relationship that he wanted to testify on our behalf rather than serve as supporting counsel. It is not imperative that your attorney believe in your position to that degree, but it helps.

In addition to telling your attorney the complete, unabridged version of the events, supplement the story with written documentation. This implies that once you enter into a relationship – any relationship that could end up in litigation – it is incumbent upon you to save *everything*. Save all written correspondence (including e-mails), all written agreements, all notes and memos that might have some evidentiary value if you ever need to reconstruct events or conversations. Save everything. The day will come when you will feel comfortable discarding the documentation, but in the meantime it provides the very best sort of insurance against lapses of memory and uncertainty over the way things happened sometime in the past.

When faced with litigation, organize the paperwork and give it to your attorney along with your written account of events. Go back over this information periodically as the process moves forward. You might be surprised at how seemingly insignificant events affect the overall story you have to tell once they are woven into the fabric of your case.

Above all, don't be afraid to offer your attorney guidance and suggestions. Your attorney knows procedure, how to prepare for the battle and how to present your case in the best possible manner. Your attorney does not know everything you know about *your* case, and never will. Keep involved and keep engaged. Don't assume your attorney can do it all without you.

PREPARING YOUR CASE

You have made the decision to go to court either to protect yourself from a spurious claim or to prosecute a claim against another. You have interviewed some attorneys and you have retained one with whom you feel comfortable. You have filed the necessary Complaint (if you are the Plaintiff) or Answer (if you are the Defendant) with the appropriate court. Now it's time to develop your case.

The process of developing a case for court is interesting and underrated. The drama of the trial might be the gripping aspect of litigation, but the credit for most success at court goes to those involved in the development of the case. Good preparation is paramount for good results.

Your lawyer and his/her legal team will bear most of the burden for the development of your case, but you should be as involved in the process as you can afford to be. The first initiative you can take is to ask questions of your attorney. Make sure you have a good understanding of how your attorney views the case and how he/she intends to proceed. Ask your counsel if there are any books or articles that he or she might recommend that will help you understand the legal process and what you will be up against in your particular case. The Internet can also be a great source of information about similar cases. There are even sites you can subscribe to that are law libraries online, where you can research state law and individual case studies. In addition, you would be well advised to visit your local courthouse and sit in on some proceedings. If you have an opportunity to watch part or all of an actual trial, take the time to do it. As boring as it might prove to be, you will no doubt develop a sense for what goes on in a courtroom. That might help you better understand the etiquette of the court and the unique vocabulary of our legal system, both of which might enable you to feel more at ease in the foreign surroundings of a courtroom.

I have spent a good deal of time in courtrooms listening to cases that had nothing to do with me. When you become involved in a lawsuit, you will probably have the opportunity (obligation, in my view) to attend many hearings that deal with the circumstances of your case, and that precede the actual trial. The hearings are scheduled to be held on days when court is in session, along with hearings that pertain to other cases. Your particular hearing might be the first one of the day or the last of the day. The clerk of court can generally offer a probable timeframe for your hearing, but not a specific start time for any given hearing. That means you will probably have an opportunity to sit in on other cases while you're awaiting your turn. It's time well spent for the educational value, and I recommend it.

Pay attention during these hearings and try to determine how you might react if you were the judge or a member of the jury.

- ✓ Are the witnesses credible?
- ✓ Does it appear that the witnesses have been well coached by their respective lawyers (i.e., they don't seem surprised by any questions)?
- ✓ Do the witnesses provide substance to the trial or is their testimony largely unnecessary, in your opinion?
- ✓ Is the evidence clear and compelling, and presented in such a way that no questions are left outstanding?

- ✓ Do the attorneys and their clients appear to be prepared and are their arguments organized and logical?
- ✓ Are they respectful of the judge and of opposing counsel?
- ✓ Are they believable, or does their body language contradict their testimony?

As you ask yourself these questions, make it a point to identify *why* your answers are what they are. If you don't believe a witness is credible, ask yourself why. If a particular attorney and client don't seem to be well prepared, ask yourself what makes you feel that way. Jot down notes, if possible, to remind you of things you want to be sure to do – or not to do – when your time comes to participate. Discuss your observations with your attorney. This learning process should continue throughout the course of your litigation.

The formal development of your case will begin with the compilation of documents and other evidence that support your side of the case and that are, in some instances, detrimental to your opponent's case. Documents might include contracts, memos, correspondence (including e-mails), photographs, and notes about (or actual transcripts of) conversations. Your personal written description of the events should be included in the documents list.

Next, you will want to identify any individuals who might be able to confirm your account of the events, either in part or in their entirety. Discuss them with your attorney and focus on the pros and cons of each potential witness. Try to determine whether they really have something beneficial to add, whether they would be credible as witnesses and whether they would be willing to testify on your behalf. This list of individuals can include "expert witnesses" – individuals who possess a particular expertise and who can help substantiate your claim(s) or perhaps help to quantify the dollar amount of any damages you may have incurred.

Special care should be taken to insure that any expert witness you might ask to testify in your case is indeed an expert in a field that is relevant to your case, and that he or she is credible. In addition, make sure you can afford their fee. Expert witnesses do not work for free. Theirs is an occupation that requires special knowledge and, quite often, many years of experience. In some circumstances, their expert knowledge might be extremely unique, and that will affect the cost of their services. Ask in advance about all fees so you are not caught unawares, and don't hesitate to interview several individuals so you are comfortable with your ultimate choice.

Once you have gathered together everything you can possibly lay your hands on that might support your case, it's time for "discovery."

Discovery is the term given to that part of case development where you ask the opposition to provide certain specific information. They are legally obligated to comply with your requests as long as they are reasonable. It is common to provide opposing counsel with the following:

- Request for Documents (listing of specific documents you want the opposing party to produce)
- Interrogatories (a list of questions to be completed by the opposing party)
- List of Individuals to be deposed (list of people you want to question under oath)

The opposing party must respond to the Request for Documents and the Interrogatories promptly and honestly, and they will expect the same from you. A response time is defined as part of the initial request, and again, it must be reasonable. Don't be surprised if the opposition requests a time extension. They often ask for additional time just to delay proceedings, and their request, if reasonable, is usually granted by the presiding judge.

Depositions might be held in one or more locations on one or more days. The attorneys for both parties will agree when and where depositions will be held and whether all parties asked to testify will be present. It is not uncommon for those being deposed to have to travel to the location where the depositions are to be held. Sometimes, the attorneys will actually travel to the individual in order to obtain a deposition. Keep in mind that the cost of all this travel is borne by the litigants. We often assume cost equals an attorney's hourly pay multiplied by the number of hours worked. Don't forget travel time and travel costs for your counsel, for certain witnesses you might call, and for individuals not directly related to the suit who you might ask to depose.

The first time I attended a deposition was in 1982 during my case with the Sowerwine family. The depositions were held in a small law office in Cody, Wyoming. I lived in Cody and was well acquainted with the place and all the players. I knew the Sowerwines, their attorney, my attorney and everyone else who was deposed during the few days of testimony. Although the process was new to me – I had never testified under oath at any prior time – I was not terribly uncomfortable because of my familiarity with the people and the surroundings.

I will admit that although I knew my facts thoroughly, I found the process of being interrogated under oath slightly intimidating at first. I quickly realized there was nothing to fear; I simply had to answer the questions asked of me, with honesty. On the advice of my attorney, I tried not to volunteer any information by elaborating on my responses unnecessarily. All in all, the process was not threatening.

I was deposed on only one other occasion – in 2006 pursuant to our 2004 suit against LSI – and things were a little different.

We began that deposition process in April of 2006. My wife, my partner and I were all deposed by LSI's counsel (all of us being shareholders in Evaluation Services, Inc.). The depositions were held at the offices of Morgan, Lewis & Bockius LLP on the 32nd floor of the One Oxford Center building in downtown Pittsburgh. The office was designed to be both imposing and intimidating by way of its location and décor. The effect was precisely as intended. A court reporter was present, as was our lone attorney and several lawyers for LSI. Gone was the sense of familiarity I had experienced in Wyoming. Here, we were clearly the outsiders. We were treated with courtesy by most (but not all) of the opposing attorneys. The atmosphere was icy.

The first person to be deposed was my wife. Although she was not, and never had been, involved in the business, she was a shareholder in our company. I had thought it proper that she, as my wife, should share in the ownership of an investment that was so important to us. I never imagined that she might be subjected to interrogation by virtue of the fact that she was a shareholder in the company.

I thought LSI's counsel was unduly harsh in their questioning of my wife. Perhaps I was just being defensive, but it was quite obvious from the beginning that she had no knowledge of events – nor should that have been expected of her. She was questioned for about an hour, and it was an hour I know she would like never to repeat. Regardless, she handled herself well. She answered those questions she could, and was honest when she couldn't provide an answer. There is no doubt in my mind that the purpose of deposing my wife was to intimidate all of us – to let us know from the start that LSI was not going to make this easy for any of us.

Despite the fact that my wife was forced to endure this discomfort, I still believe her ownership in the company is both important and prudent from the perspective of family financial planning. I don't mean to discourage the practice by telling this story. I do hope that the telling of it helps other realize that any ownership in a business enterprise exposes one to the potential involvement in litigation. That is not to be feared, but it should be understood.

The remaining depositions – mine and my partner's – were conducted over the next day and a half. The questioning was not friendly, and at times both we and LSI's attorneys became agitated with one another. The experience was vastly different from my first deposition in Wyoming several years earlier. I was in control of the facts, but LSI's counsel was clearly in control of the process. My interrogator was skillful at switching subject matter, posing identical questions in different ways and creating in me a sense of uncertainty. It was a real grilling.

The intent, of course, was to get me to say something that might contradict a statement I had made earlier or to represent a single event in a manner dissimilar to the way I had previously described it. My partner was put to the same test and was asked many of the same questions I had been asked, in the hope that he might offer up different responses.

Within days of the conclusion of our depositions, we received the written transcripts of our testimony to review and acknowledge as accurate representations of the conversations that took place. Only then did we have a good opportunity to review the questions and answers thoroughly in order to determine if we had misspoken at any time.

I believe it is virtually impossible to undergo a lengthy interrogation by a well-trained inquisitor without making a misstatement somewhere along the way. My partner and I both discovered instances where our answers were either incomplete or perhaps unclear. There was a place or two where it was obvious by our answers that we had misunderstood the questions. We made notations of those, knowing full well some of our misstatements would be used against us later on.

This is a good place to mention that it is imperative that you read your deposition carefully. Not only do you need to be aware of any errors or misstatements you made, but you also need to check for errors made by the court reporter. Court reporters are unbelievably good at what they do. They sit for hours listening to testimony and transcribing conversations word for word. However, they are human and they do make mistakes. One word misunderstood and placed in the middle of a sentence can change the entire context of the statement.

As an example, during my deposition for the 2004 suit against LSI, I said, "So when you *take* all of that information ..." When I read the draft furnished by the court reporter, I found the sentence had been transcribed as, "So when you *fake* all of that information ..." Big difference. Huge difference! I corrected the text, and the final copy furnished to the court by the stenographer contained the proper wording. You can't change what you did say, but you certainly have a right – an obligation – to correct what you didn't say. Read the deposition carefully.

LSI did try to weave a couple of our misstatements into their arguments in briefs they filed subsequent to the depositions. I don't believe their attempts had any substantial effect. We had expected these attacks, and our attorney had prepared appropriate responses even before they appeared in any court documents. For the most part, we had known our facts, and we were clear in our understanding of LSI's breaches. Our depositions had served their proper purpose: they had helped to establish the facts of the case.

During the early stages of our preparation for the case against LSI, we (our attorney, my partner and I) tried to determine if there were one or more witnesses who might help our cause. Our Colorado attorney, who had been involved in our dealings with LSI since 1995, had already asked to testify. He was absolutely incensed by LSI's conduct over the years and wanted to give evidence about his first-hand experience with LSI's attorneys. We knew he would make an excellent witness and planned to take him up on his offer.

There was only one other person, besides me and my partner, whose testimony we thought would be useful. I will call him Jerry. He had been in charge of LSI's automated valuation initiative from 2000 until the sale of LSI to Fidelity National Financial in 2003. He had always been sympathetic to our predicament; he himself had voiced disgust with LSI's business practices on numerous occasions. After the sale of LSI, Jerry continued to work in Fidelity's automated valuation division and his office was still located in the LSI building in Pittsburgh. We thought he would be willing to step forward as an honest and credible witness because during our days at LSI he had often joked that he would be our star witness if and when we finally sued LSI. We also believed he might be able to corroborate our claims without implicating himself. We were certain he had shared no part in directing LSI's bad faith conduct; as a junior officer, he was probably unaware of many of LSI's management decisions that affected our relationship.

Jerry was the only person we deposed in April of 2006. The interview began pleasantly enough. I greeted him and he greeted me, although he did seem to be nervous and uptight. Once we got beyond the introductory questions ("please state your name and address for the record") it became apparent that Jerry was not going to provide any beneficial testimony. I suppose he was afraid of jeopardizing his job. Regardless, he refused to answer most of the questions my attorney posed – "I don't remember" was his standard response. Although we made every attempt to pry some information out of him, Jerry was steadfast. Having made a reasonable effort to encourage him to testify openly and honestly, we gave up. On the way out I thanked him and told him it was fortunate he had remembered his name and address. Otherwise he would have been unable to respond to *any* of our questions.

Although Jerry could have provided some extremely useful information, he chose not to. It serves no purpose to excoriate him in this text; I'm certain LSI's attorneys had made very clear what was expected of him. His testimony (or lack thereof) was a disappointment and a real blow to our case. Jerry was the only "insider" who had knowledge of the events and a grasp of the facts sufficient to damage LSI's defense. I selfishly wish he had shown more backbone, but we've all had times when we wish we had stood taller.

We learned one important thing from Jerry's deposition and that was that he would not be a suitable witness at trial. Sometimes what people won't tell you turns out to be as significant as what they will tell you.

This, of course, is one of the reasons that depositions are taken. The first reason is to nail down the facts of the case. The information that can be gained from individuals testifying under oath can help fill in blanks in the record of events. The second reason is to determine who might and might not be a good witness at trial.

In contrast to this unfortunate experience, we very much enjoyed the private interview with our designated expert witness that we arranged about this same time. We realized early on that we would need an expert to help legitimize the amount of damages we were asking the court to award. There were few people who could adequately fill that position because the industry for which our Software was designed – the automated property valuation business – was relatively new. It was therefore difficult to assess how much income we might have been able to generate if LSI had delivered the Software to us when it was first required of them in 1997. That, of course, would serve as the basis for our lost profits, which in turn would be the basis for our request for damages.

My partner and I were among the most knowledgeable individuals in the industry and had a very good understanding of what we had lost. To our surprise, so did our expert witness. In addition to being a business valuation expert, she was an actual real estate appraiser who – as chance would have it – had been in the appraisal business in Colorado in the 1990s. Since our property valuation business had been confined to the State of Colorado, her familiarity with that market was of extreme importance. She also had a good deal of prior experience testifying as an expert witness. Her appearance was pleasant, her knowledge was extensive, and her demeanor was credible. She was perfect.

Thus ended the witness selection and deposition portions of the development of our case. Much of the information we gleaned from this exercise was incorporated into briefs filed with the court and statements made at formal hearings. Although we never got to trial, we certainly felt as though we were well prepared for the eventuality.

During the Sowerwine lawsuit in 1983 we actually did go to trial. We had our documentary evidence in order and our witnesses were ready to go. Before trial began, however, we spent time developing a list of questions we wanted to ask each of our witnesses and each of the other camp's witnesses in order to allow a true and correct account of the events to unfold in an orderly fashion. With each of our witnesses, we shared a list of those questions we intended to ask of them. One of the rules of litigation is that you should never ask a question of anyone in a courtroom without knowing how they will respond. From the information we had accumulated at depositions, we knew how each of the witnesses for the opposition would testify, assuming their testimony at court corresponded with their testimony at deposition. We were not worried about the possibility that their testimony might differ from what they had previously said under oath. If it did, their credibility would be suspect, and their courtroom testimony would probably have little import.

Our primary responsibility was to make certain that our witnesses remained true to their prior testimony, if they had been deposed. If they had not testified under oath prior to the trial, we wanted to go over our questions with them beforehand, as well as those likely to be posed by opposing counsel. We didn't want them to be surprised by any unexpected questions; it was important that they should feel as comfortable and prepared for the trial as we did.

We also organized our evidence and our witness list by order of appearance so that our account of events and the facts we provided to support that account had a logical flow. At court, the story you tell must be clear, concise and compelling. There is no substitute for the organization that precedes the actual presentation of the facts and testimony at court.

I was personally called to testify during the Sowerwine trial, and I was *very* well prepared. I knew my facts, and was a resolute witness. In retrospect, my testimony probably came across as being curt – not impolite, but not congenial either. I answered every question posed by my counsel and those offered up by opposing counsel during cross examination with alacrity and determination. If I had any sense of humility in my mid 30s, it was not on display at trial. I wanted the judge to know that I was the damaged party and that I had no regard for Sowerwine, his attorney, or their tactics. My demeanor, in all probability, did not work in my favor. Although I was neither disrespectful nor uncooperative, I was perhaps a little too tough.

Looking back, I think the judge probably understood how I felt. I didn't need to parade my anger in front of him.

Given the opportunity to testify again, I would approach the witness stand with a different purpose. I would certainly be as well prepared, and I would try to impress the court with my command of the facts – not my distaste for my opponent(s). I think the way you present yourself at court does influence the way the court (judge or jury) sees you. If you appear to be level-headed rather than hot-headed and knowledgeable instead of a know-it-all, I think it will serve you well.

THE TRUTH, THE WHOLE TRUTH AND NOTHING BUT THE TRUTH

I wasn't really surprised the first time a witness told a lie in order to support my opponent's case against me. I was disappointed, but not surprised. Since then I have listened to the sworn testimony of numerous witnesses at deposition and at trial, and have been appalled at how insignificant the threat of perjury is to folks who have an agenda. I hope no one has ever given false testimony on my account.

At some point during my lawsuit with the Sowerwines, I received a call at my home from an individual with whom I was not acquainted, asking if I would meet him at a local coffee shop. He had something he wanted to talk with me about. Out of curiosity I went. I was met by three individuals who professed to have elaborate plans for the development of the Sowerwine property. They had apparently been engaged in conversation with E.O. Sowerwine, Jr. about the prospect of developing a portion of his ranchland some years earlier, and they wanted to know if I might be interested in "partnering" with them now that I owned the land. Their view of a partnership was that I would put up the land and some development money, they would contribute the plan, and we would split the income. I politely excused myself and told them I was not interested in developing the land under any circumstances.

I was totally surprised when one of these individuals was called to testify a few months later during the trial. What in the world could this fellow add that had any value? To my surprise he testified that he had met with me, and I had told him and his associates that I had planned to steal Sowerwine's property from him. I had said nothing of the sort. My immediate thought was that Sowerwine must have promised that, if successful at court, he would participate in this disreputable soul's development scheme in return for his bogus testimony. Here was a character of incredibly poor character impugning my character! I was incensed.

On cross examination my attorney made every attempt to discredit the witness, but who knows how this false testimony might have hurt my case. The judge had to decide whether to believe me or this individual who was, to that point in the trial, virtually unknown to anyone connected with the case except Sowerwine and his attorney. Whether this false testimony impacted the judge's decision one way or the other is really unimportant now, but it is a blatant example of a witness lying with deliberation, under oath.

Attorneys lie too. I have heard them make false statements in court and have witnessed their false statements in written filings. On a very few occasions I have seen attorneys be forced to withdraw false statements, but I have never heard one apologize for making a false statement.

In their brief in support of their Motion for Summary Judgment, LSI's counsel included a section entitled "Statement of Undisputed Facts." For several pages, they enumerated a number of "facts," some of which were factual and some of which were not. Among those items that were improperly included as facts was the following statement:

In November 2002, after lengthy negotiations, the parties resolved these disputes and entered into the Release (Settlement & Release Agreement). Plaintiffs ... agreed to *release all of their claims against LSI in exchange for an increased royalty rate and "guaranteed minimum annual royalties" of $50,000 for seven years.*

The statement was absolutely false. The actual – *factual* – language of the Release specified:

It is further expressly understood and agreed that the consideration recited herein together with the increase in the royalty rate described in the Third Amendment to the Software Purchase Agreement and the release of the non-competition provision described in the Second Amendment to the Consulting Agreement is the only consideration for this Release and that this document recites all the terms and conditions of settlement.

The brief prepared by LSI's counsel was silent with regard to their client's obligation to provide *the release of the non-competition provision* as consideration, but the Release Agreement had certainly been specific about it. LSI had avoided mentioning this in their brief because they had failed to provide the release, despite the contractual requirement that they do so. They did make a comment later in the brief that we were alleging LSI had breached the Release Agreement "by failing to waive in a timely manner a non-compete provision in the Consulting Agreement." That was not exactly accurate either. We claimed the Release Agreement was *invalid* because LSI had failed to deliver the release of the non-compete provision that was specifically set forth as part of the consideration we were to have received. There's a big difference between saying someone breached an agreement and saying that someone's actions have rendered an agreement invalid and unenforceable (therefore unable to be breached). LSI's lawyers apparently had real trouble acknowledging to the court that their client had been obligated to provide this additional consideration, and had failed to do so.

Sometimes people don't really lie. Sometimes they honestly can't remember what happened or their recollection is simply incorrect, and the testimony they give is, therefore, incorrect. After all, by the time a dispute has festered to the point where litigation is the only apparent option, a good deal of time may have passed. It is understandable that people become fuzzy on the exact circumstances of a case – even those individuals most directly involved. None of us has perfect recall of events. However, sometimes people forget or fail to remember events as they were, on purpose. I think they believe they are not really lying if they fudge a little here or there. If they say they can't remember instead of telling a truth that might hurt the side they are representing, it doesn't seem as bad as lying. It is.

Then there's the half truth. This is a statement that is essentially factual, but that tells only part of the whole truth. In their reply to our Complaint, LSI's attorneys filled pages with half truths designed to give a whole different meaning to a set of facts. Here's an example.

In countering our claim that LSI had caused us to lose income by failing and refusing to deliver the Software to us as per the terms of the Software License Agreements, LSI's counsel stated that we should be barred from collecting damages because we had made no attempt to acquire other Software or develop new Software to replace that which LSI had failed to give us. The argument in and of itself sounded pretty feeble, but what the attorneys did not tell the court was that we *couldn't* acquire or develop other Software. The original Purchase Agreement contained a provision that stated we would not compete with LSI in the automated valuation business for eight years after the effective date of the purchase, with the exception that we could use the Software to continue our ongoing valuation business in the State of Colorado. We promised not to work for anyone else who performed automated valuations, and we promised not to acquire or develop another automated valuation model until the expiration of the covenant not to compete. LSI's attorneys had stated a true fact when they said we had not made an effort to acquire or develop another piece of valuation Software, but they failed to disclose to the court that we could do neither because we had promised LSI – in a contract – that we wouldn't. They had told a half truth, and that half truth had the effect of altering the real truth. Americans have become so accustomed to this trick that we have created a term for it: "spin." We hear spin every day from our politicians, from the CEOs of major corporations, from newscasters. We seldom read anything newsworthy that is not the product of spin. We have come to accept it, and only the most inquisitive among us question it. Yet when spin crosses the line and becomes prevarication – as it often does – it becomes more than misleading. It becomes dangerous and harmful.

In the instance just cited, we of course set the record straight by explaining the terms of the non-compete covenant. That didn't stop LSI's attorneys from continuing to use this defense. It seems that one theory at court is that if you say something often enough, the judge and/or jury will believe it, whether it is factual or not. If this happens to you, rebut false claims and statements each and every time they come up. If you don't, you might find these phony claims recited in a judge's decision as statements of fact.

As harmful and as shocking as the outright lie, is the innuendo. I've heard opposing counsel use this ploy more often than witnesses, but either way it strikes me as a criminal abuse. It's the snide remark made offhand that doesn't allow for a reply, or the way a question is phrased to imply impropriety, or the false sense of surprise uttered by the lawyer who wants the court to question the testimony of a witness. All these tactics and theatrics are allowed, but inappropriate in my opinion.

Don't be surprised if you fall prey to this sort of tactic. If possible, talk with your attorney at your first opportunity and ask if it is appropriate for your attorney to cover the same ground, allowing you the chance to give a proper and complete response. Your attorney might not think it's worth doing, but trust your gut. You have a say in how things pertaining to your case are handled. If you think the opposing counsel has damaged your credibility with spurious remarks and/or a line of questioning designed to impugn your reliability, tell your attorney you want to set the record straight. However, be specific as to what you intend to accomplish and what questions you would like your attorney to ask. This is that relationship thing. If you and your attorney work together well and trust each other, you can identify damage when it occurs and make every effort to repair it – together.

You might be surprised to hear me say that judges are sometimes less than truthful. "Blasphemy!" you say. I must admit it was difficult for me to believe that a judge might lie. I understood that a judge might view the circumstances surrounding an event differently than I, and therefore might arrive at a very different conclusion. We all have our biases that cause us to see things from slightly different perspectives. That's normal and understandable. However, I wasn't prepared to accept the fact that a judge might arrive at a decision for some inappropriate reason, and support that decision with a "results-based" opinion – one that has been fashioned to support the decision regardless of whether it has any foundation in law or in fact.

At the epicenter of our case against LSI loomed a Settlement & Release Agreement, to which I have referred earlier. In November of the year 2002, we executed this agreement promising that we would not bring suit against LSI for most of our numerous past grievances, including LSI's failure to perform some of its obligations under the terms of the Software License Agreements. In exchange for this promise, LSI was to increase our software royalties (which they did) and provide us with a release of our covenant not to compete that had been executed in 1997 concurrent with the sale of the Software to LSI (which they did not). As it turned out, LSI was sold to Fidelity National Financial within 60 days of our execution of this agreement and the increased royalties quickly evaporated – Fidelity said it had its own valuation system and saw no need to use ours, which required the payment of royalties. We were left without any royalty income, and without the ability to participate in the industry I had founded because LSI refused to release us from our covenant not to compete.

When we brought suit against LSI in 2004, LSI countered that we should be barred from suing them for their transgressions because we had executed the Settlement & Release Agreement promising we wouldn't sue them. They ignored the fact they had failed to fully compensate us for our pledge by releasing us from our non-compete agreement, as called for in the Settlement & Release Agreement.

We raised this issue at Court. We specifically asked the judge to rule on the validity of the Settlement & Release Agreement, contending that it was unenforceable because LSI had failed to provide the full consideration they had promised. Our contention was based on the basic legal principal that an offer and acceptance alone do not create a valid and binding contract. A third element, *consideration, must* exist. Without consideration, an offer and acceptance represent merely a naked, unenforceable promise.

Judge Scanlon failed to address the validity of the Agreement, and instead simply ruled that the case should be dismissed as a consequence of the Settlement & Release Agreement. When forced to make mention of the Agreement in the edification of his opinion that was filed with the Superior Court of Pennsylvania pursuant to our Appeal, Scanlon defended his avoidance of the matter, saying:

"Accordingly, the November 2002 Release acts to bar at a minimum the claims pertaining to the royalties and the "LSI only" [Internet based] *valuations, and summary judgment was appropriate."*

Judge Scanlon spoke to the intent of the Agreement but failed to address the issue we raised regarding the validity and enforceability of the Release Agreement. Obviously, if the Release was determined to be invalid – and without full consideration being tendered there is no other way to interpret the validity of the Release – then Judge Scanlon's opinion fails. He chose to ignore the issue.

Now you might not call that "lying"; however, if it isn't lying I don't know what you *would* call it. It wasn't an oversight; it was a deliberate avoidance of the issue – an issue that was at the very center of the dispute.

We appealed Judge Scanlon's decision to the Pennsylvania Superior Court. The Superior Court assembles panels, each composed of three judges, to hear cases at argument. Our case was heard by Judges Johnson, Tamilia and Melvin on June 27, 2007. In our appeal we again raised the issue of the validity of the Settlement & Release Agreement. We devoted pages to subject, giving it thorough explanation and citing appropriate case law. We concluded that:

Because part of the consideration for the settlement failed to pass from LSI to ESI, the Settlement & Release Agreement suffers a "failure of consideration."

The conclusion – that the Settlement & Release Agreement was unenforceable – was afforded high visibility in the brief, and again we asked to court to make a specific ruling on this most important matter.

The Superior Court, like Judge Scanlon, failed to address the issue at all. Instead, they confirmed Judge Scanlon's opinion and basically blew us off. We immediately filed a Petition for Reargument, trying to compel the court to respond to our pointed demand that they address the validity of the Agreement. We knew full well that if the court would admit the Agreement was invalid, we could proceed to trial and force our claim against LSI.

According to the Rules of Court for the Pennsylvania Superior Court, we had the option of filing a Petition for Reconsideration with the three judges who heard the initial argument, or a Motion for Reargument which would be submitted to the full Court – all 22 judges. Whether or not either petition is granted is up to the discretion of the Court; neither is a matter of right, and there are only certain prescribed circumstances under which a Petition will be granted.

We opted to file an Application for Reargument on the basis that the panel who heard our argument overlooked a material fact of record that could have substantially altered their decision. That approach enabled us to provide a copy of our petition to each of the 22 judges on the Superior Court. We thought it would be more difficult for the entire Court to ignore the panel's error than it might be for the original panel to simply deny a request for reconsideration.

Our Motion for Reconsideration/Application for Reargument was denied on December 6, 2007. The denial wasn't even signed by a judge. It bore the signature of the Deputy Prothonotary (the principal clerk of the court).

I was again at a loss for a way to characterize the court's action. Was their ruling a deceitful document? Was it a lie? They avoided the central issue that would have turned their opinion upside down, and they obviously did so in order to justify their ruling. Their opinion was not based on the facts of the case, but was fashioned to support the outcome they preferred. I don't know about you, but I call that lying.

In January of 2008, we filed an appeal with the Supreme Court of the State of Pennsylvania. We hoped they would have the integrity to hear the case and to give serious consideration to the obvious "oversight" of the lower courts. We were sorely disappointed when on October 1, 2008 they issued an order denying our appeal.

YOU CAN'T PREDICT THE OUTCOME

If I were to have been asked to predict the outcome of any of the lawsuits I have been involved in, I would have said:

"Given a fair hearing before a fair, honest and competent judge, we will win."

Interestingly, even knowing the actual outcomes, I would give the same response today. However, I now know the reality: There is no way to predict the outcome of a court case. There are too many variables. First, the facts of any case are seldom black and white. Even if the facts are black and white, an experienced attorney can turn them a shade of gray in a brief or an oral presentation. In addition, unexpected things happen. A witness might drop a bombshell in the form of a comment that undermines the very heart of the case; a plaintiff or a defendant might be so uncomfortable on the stand that their testimony comes across as being suspect; a judge might be having a bad day and pay little attention to the critical issues of the case. Any number, or any combination, of things could converge to create a surprise ending to a case everyone thought would be resolved a certain way. I have found that out the hard way.

Sowerwine vs. Stockton (1982)

In my case with the Sowerwines, there was no contractual issue. Neither party was claiming any breach of contract – the option term had simply expired. The only matter before the court was whether I had impeded Sowerwine's ability to obtain the financing necessary for him to comply with the terms of the Agreement and Option to Repurchase.

Sowerwine claimed that I had intentionally violated the covenant of Good Faith & Fair Dealing that governs contracts – specifically, that I had prevented him from obtaining a loan by virtue of using my "influence" in the banking community, and by my bad faith conduct in my dealings with Sowerwine himself.

I had been a banker in Wyoming for a number of years prior to the time I purchased the property from Sowerwine's father. Although I remained on the Board of Directors of a small bank in southern Wyoming, I was not actively engaged in banking when the Agreement and Option to Repurchase was executed. At the time, the population of Wyoming was hovering around 350,000 people and the banking community was quite small. I was acquainted with many of the state's bankers but maintained that I had not interfered with Sowerwine's loan applications in any way.

Unbeknownst to me, Sowerwine had made loan requests of several local lenders just before the expiration of the one-year repurchase period – a sort of last-minute blitz. He had apparently received encouragement from the Federal Land Bank where he had been told that if he could find interim financing to complete the repurchase, they might be willing to grant him a permanent loan. In my experience as a banker, I recognized that "non-commitment" as a way of dismissing a would-be borrower with whom you don't want to do business. However, based on his discussions with the Land Bank, Sowerwine had submitted applications to at least two of the three local Cody, Wyoming banks. He had also applied to the Stockgrowers State Bank in Worland, Wyoming, 80 miles distant – the bank that held my mortgage on the property, but with which Sowerwine had no prior relationship. I was aware of the tentative commitment from the Land Bank – Sowerwine had mentioned it during our meeting held June 12, 1982 – but I was totally unaware of his efforts to obtain interim financing from area banks.

On Monday, June 14th, 1982, having met with Sowerwine and determined he was not going to be able to repurchase the property, I met with my banker at Stockgrowers State Bank to make application to renew my loan. The loan was due and payable on June 22nd – the date by which Sowerwine had to tender the repurchase money – and that left me little more than a week for the bank's loan committee to evaluate my request for a renewal. At the meeting with my banker, I disclosed to him that since the original loan had been made, I had discovered that there was a restrictive covenant on the property that banned the raising of livestock. When I had purchased the ranch a year earlier, I had anticipated leasing out part of the land for livestock grazing as a means of generating income to repay my loan. About 60 days prior to my meeting with the bank, my attorney had determined the covenant banning livestock was valid and binding, and I was obligated to disclose the fact to the bank. Had Sowerwine repurchased the property, the presence of the covenant would not have been an issue. At the time of my request to renew the loan, this was a pertinent issue.

At trial, Sowerwine's attorney called on several bankers to testify. They were all employed by banks to which Sowerwine had applied for financing. To a man, they stated they had never discussed those applications with me and affirmed that I had not influenced their decisions to deny Sowerwine's request. The Sowerwines had been denied solely on the basis of their abysmal credit history. A loan officer for Stockgrowers State Bank testified that at the time Sowerwine's application was under consideration there was a brief discussion about the matter of the restrictive covenant (Sowerwine had not disclosed it them, but I had in my application), and some of the loan committee members had expressed concern. However, according to the bank's president, Sowerwine's application had been denied solely for credit reasons. In fact, as he left the witness stand, he whispered to me and my attorney, "I wouldn't have loaned him the money if he'd given me a gold-plated application." I have often wished he'd had the fortitude to make that same strong statement on the witness stand.

Sowerwine's attorney made much of my disclosure regarding the covenant, implying it was a deliberate effort to undermine his client's loan request. In reply I said it was my obligation to disclose the matter to my banker at the time of my application for refinancing. I also asked why I would have had any reason to believe Sowerwine would make application to my bank – a bank far removed from his community and one with which he had never done business. Finally, I suggested that Sowerwine had acted with impropriety by not disclosing the matter of the covenant in his own loan request.

The trial ended on a Friday afternoon and the attorneys for both parties were instructed to prepare closing arguments in writing and submit them to the court in the coming days. We waited the better part of a year for the judge to hand down his ruling.

In his conclusion, Judge Dixon said,

"The actions of the Defendant (me), *taken singly, may appear justified and consistent with the actions of an individual protecting his own interests. But when considered as a whole, Defendant's actions display a conscious, methodical obstructive course of action toward the Plaintiff and his attempts to exercise the option and such actions resulted in the actual hindrance of the Plaintiff."*

He continued:

"Plaintiff has established sufficient equitable grounds to excuse his failure to timely exercise his option and he is entitled to equitable relief from this Court."

This was an interesting – if not questionable – ruling. By doing what I was obligated to do and nothing more, my actions were judged to be damaging. By failing to perform, but claiming that my inaction had prevented him from doing what the agreement demanded of him, he was judged to have complied sufficiently to be granted equitable relief.

The specific actions "taken singly" that the judge referred to were enumerated in the judge's decision:

- ✓ I and my attorney refused to accept the assignment of the Agreement and Option to Repurchase from E.O., Jr. to E.O. III because the Broken H Ranch Trust, a party to the Agreement and Option to Repurchase, was not a party to the assignment.
    - o To do otherwise would have been foolhardy.

- ✓ I refused Sowerwine's request for more time to round up the option money.
    - o I was under no obligation to do so. I did offer to consider his request if he was willing to offer additional compensation. He was not.

- ✓ I refused to have the property surveyed without Sowerwine first delivering the certified funds as required by the Agreement.
    - o I wasn't about to spend money on a survey needlessly, nor was I going to do anything that might alter the terms of the Agreement as written.

- ✓ I disclosed the presence of a restrictive covenant to my banker at the time I applied for a renewal of my loan, as required by law and conscience.
    - o The judge elected to interpret that disclosure as a deliberate attempt to encourage the Stockgrowers State Bank to deny Sowerwine's loan request, despite the fact that I didn't know Sowerwine had made application to the bank.

It strikes me that all of the actions the judge enumerated were reasonable and responsible – taken singly *and* as a whole.

Regardless, the judge ruled in Sowerwine's favor and then added an unusual twist. He unilaterally rewrote our contract that had been forged back in 1981. He gave Sowerwine an additional four months to try to raise the repurchase money – this in addition to the fifteen months that had already transpired since Sowerwine had defaulted due to non-payment. In addition, he decided that Sowerwine should not have to reimburse me for the interest that was accruing on my mortgage beyond the initial option date in June of 1982 – an amount that was substantial given the fact that mortgage rates at the time were in excess of 18%. The judge further ordered that in the event Sowerwine tendered the repurchase monies within the extended time period, I was to deed the property back to him within five days – regardless of whether or not I intended to appeal the judge's ruling. If I failed to do so, the judge would direct the court to issue Sowerwine a deed, and I would be deprived of the profits and the five acres the contract guaranteed me. I would be left without any profit, any property, and with a significant debt.

Even without legal training, I harbored serious doubts that a judge could unilaterally rewrite a contract between parties. It had been my belief that a judge had to interpret a contract literally unless the contract was ambiguous. This contract was not ambiguous, and had not come under scrutiny during the trial. I argued with my attorney that the judge's ruling was "illegal"; he couldn't do that. My attorney agreed, but commented, "He just did."

On October 11, 1983, my attorney filed a motion demanding that the original terms of the Agreement and Option to Repurchase be upheld or, in the alternative, I be granted a new trial on the grounds that "the conclusion and judgment are contrary to law." Judge Dixon denied the motion on both counts.

I did indeed file an appeal with the Wyoming Supreme Court, and when Sowerwine delivered the repurchase money to the Stockgrowers State Bank in December of 1983, I refused to execute a deed granting him the property, on advice of counsel. Where would I be if I won the appeal? Would I have to initiate another suit against Sowerwine to regain ownership of the property? Both my attorney and I agreed that deeding the property back to Sowerwine prior to the ruling by the Wyoming Supreme Court could be a big mistake.

In May of 1984, Judge Dixon ordered that the property – all 1510 acres – be deeded to E.O. Sowerwine III by the court. He acknowledged that my appeal of his judgment had been perfected on December 29, 1983, and was pending review by the Wyoming Supreme Court. However, he maintained that his court retained jurisdiction over the matter. He directed the court to deed the property to Sowerwine in its entirety, and he denied me the compensation I was assured by our contract. The purchase agreement I had entered into in 1981 and that I viewed as being an ironclad arrangement that guaranteed me a profit, had been rewritten by a judge and had subsequently cost me a couple of hundred thousand dollars in interest, attorney fees and lost time.

The Supreme Court did eventually uphold the ruling of the lower court. Their decision was a simple statement unaccompanied by explanation; I don't know if they ever seriously considered my appeal. The conclusion was that the presiding judge at District Court had the best opportunity to see and hear all the evidence in the case, and that his ability to weigh the facts of the case should not be questioned. Case closed.

I disagreed then and disagree now with Judge Dixon's decision and with the Supreme Court's ratification of that decision. Sowerwine's failure to tender the repurchase money on time was in no way impacted by my actions, and I should have been allowed to retain the property. Regardless, in my opinion and in the opinion of my counsel, Judge Dixon had erred on a much deeper level; he had violated existing law by setting aside the terms of a contract that was never in dispute and imposing new terms of his own manufacture. We never had an opportunity to dispute these new terms before a higher authority, because those terms developed over the course of several months even as our appeal to the Wyoming Supreme Court was moving forward.

I have often wondered how this decision might have affected future litigants who had this new legal precedent applied to their cases, for the judge had essentially created new law by virtue of his ruling. He had intentionally or inadvertently created a precedent for a judge to alter the terms of an existing contract that was not a subject of dispute between the parties to the contract. Judges are supposed to apply the law; however, there can be a fine line between the interpretation of a law and the inadvertent creation of new law. I will add that this sort of thing happens more frequently than you might imagine.

Going back to the statement I made at the beginning of this section, the implication of this account is that I did *not* receive "a fair hearing before a fair, honest and competent judge." I'd have to stand by that conclusion. Perhaps this particular judge, who was universally known to dislike the Sowerwine family, had tried to show the world he could set aside his differences and find in favor of a known adversary. Perhaps he was simply incompetent. Regardless, I was thunderstruck by the ruling and the subsequent Supreme Court decision. I could have never predicted the outcome.

When I think back on this experience I am reminded of Richard Lawrence's attempt to assassinate President Andrew Jackson in 1835. Jackson was walking across the Capitol Rotunda when Lawrence walked up to him, aimed a pistol at him at point blank range, and fired. The gun misfired, whereupon Lawrence – prepared for any eventuality – drew a second pistol and fired once again. As fate would have it, that gun also misfired, allowing the 67-year-old Jackson to retaliate with his cane. Jackson was quickly restrained and Lawrence was captured. He was subsequently deemed insane and institutionalized.

He could have never predicted that outcome.

WATCH YOUR BACKSIDE

The "gamesmanship" involved in litigation often overshadows the salient issues being litigated. It is not unusual for an adversary to try to make his opponent's life so miserable that the case is simply dropped out of fear of legal or financial consequences. This happened in both of my cases against LSI.

During the primary case filed in 2004, LSI asked the court to award them legal fees should they prevail in their Motion for Summary Judgment. They estimated their costs to be in excess of $360,000. Before the hearing on the Motion, there was a good deal of discomfort in our camp; the concern over the prospect of being forced to reimburse LSI for such outrageous costs was incredibly intimidating to all of us. I got through the moment because I believed so strongly in our case that I thought the court would rule in our favor and dismiss the Motion. I also believed that, in the event the ruling went against us, no reasonable judge would grant such an unmerited request for reimbursement. Knowing what I now know, I was perhaps a bit naïve. Sometimes ignorance really is bliss.

Regardless, LSI's tactic worked to a degree. The court did indeed rule in LSI's favor on the Motion for Summary Judgment, and our case was thrown out of court. However, the judge refused to grant LSI's request for reimbursement of reasonable costs. Despite that decision, my partner was so unsettled by LSI's continued demand that the court provide them relief in the form of reimbursement that he refused to carry the fight any further. We were able to come to an accommodation that allowed me to move forward with an appeal, but the damage LSI intended had been done, if only partially. My wife and I were left to carry on the fight alone, with great personal resolve, but also with diminished resources. LSI succeeded in winning not only at the Court of Common Pleas, but also in the psyches of some of its detractors. Pure gamesmanship.

LSI never was able to convince the court they should be entitled to any reimbursement.

In the case we filed against LSI in 2006, the same tactic was employed. Both at the Court of Common Pleas and again at the Superior Court level, LSI demanded reimbursement for its costs of litigation, claiming our suit was frivolous – designed only to cause LSI grief. Their request was denied by both courts.

Following the decision by the Superior Court – at the same time we were filing our appeal to the Supreme Court – LSI filed a motion asking the Superior Court to remand the issue of their request for reasonable fees back to the lower court for consideration. In their motion (entitled "Application of Appellee for Further Costs"), they claimed our "relentless legal crusade does not excuse (their) abuse of the judicial system." Pretty strong stuff.

It was immediately apparent that it was LSI's motion and not our claim that was frivolous. The Superior Court's decision regarding our claim had come down as a formal opinion. The Court intended to, and indeed did, publish the opinion for precedential citation. As a matter of course, those opinions that speak to important legal issues or that are considered worthy of serving as future reference because they establish precedent, are published in official reports. Almost by definition, cases for which court opinions are published are substantive – not frivolous.

LSI's motion was designed to cause me consternation; I don't believe they ever expected the court to take the action they requested. By filing their motion, LSI knew my counsel would have to file an appropriate response, and that would cost me both time and money. They continued to hope that by "piling on," they could convince me to simply drop the case and forgo any further appeals. Their plan didn't work, but their tactic was nonetheless fruitful. It did cost me time. I had to consider the situation and discuss the possible outcome with my attorney. I had to pay my attorney for his consultation as well as for the time he spent formulating a reply to the court and his costs associated with the new filing. While I was not the least bit inclined to fold my cards, I did find LSI's continued snipes tiresome and aggravatingly costly.

I mention these experiences because once litigation begins, you can expect your opponent to use any and all legitimate tactics to encourage you to pack your bags and go home – for good. If you can be persuaded to drop out of the game, your adversary's path to success is assured, and the cost of success is reduced.

I don't mean to imply that there are not times when you should consider dropping a suit or attempting to settle outside of court. You always have to be realistic about your chances of succeeding and open to alternative approaches, such as settlement. However, whatever course your litigation takes, be mindful that your opponent will very likely use tactics designed to discourage you from pressing a demand or to encourage you to settle. Just watch your backside.

WHAT DO YOU DO WHEN YOU LOSE?

When a decision goes against you at court, you do have a right to an appeal. It becomes your decision whether an appeal is justified. You have to consider the cost of the appeal, the amount of time it might take, and the odds that the appeal will result in a more favorable decision. I can tell you what experience and counsel have taught me: An appeal is an uphill battle.

Before you rush to appeal the court's ruling out of a sense of outrage at the decision that has been rendered, I suggest you take a couple of intermediate steps. First, review the decision carefully. If it is incomplete – simply a thumbs down decision that is unsupported – consider filing a request for clarification. You have the right to know *why* the court ruled against you. If you don't know why, there isn't much you can appeal. We had to file requests for clarification in both our suits against LSI because the judges' decisions were not accompanied by explanations. Here's the decision we received from Judge Scanlon on June 27, 2006:

ORDER OF COURT

AND NOW, this 26th day of June 2006, following argument, and after review of the entire record, the Summary Judgment Motion of Defendant, Lender's Services, Inc., is hereby GRANTED.

That sure doesn't tell you much. By contrast, Judge Scanlon's reply to our request for clarification was 22 pages in length. It was the information in the reply that we needed – not a dismissive statement.

In the event the court provided an explanation, but you have serious problems with the reasoning because:

a. a point of law has been overlooked, or

b. one or more essential facts have been overlooked,

you can ask the court to reconsider the ruling. It is rare indeed for a court to overturn its own decision. However, by asking, you have made your concern part of the official record of the case, and at appeal that could be significant – for two reasons.

First, if the lower court has overlooked or misstated a fact and if you don't challenge their error, it will be considered fact by the appellate court. I know that sounds odd, but uncontested statements – even false statements – can be construed as facts by an appellate court. If they are uncontested, what option does the appellate court really have? Second, by focusing attention on a significant oversight, the appellate court will (or should) find it difficult to ignore the matter.

The kernel of wisdom here is simply that one should never bow to the court. If you feel like you have been denied justice because of procedural missteps or because facts were overlooked or misinterpreted, make an issue of it. It might not do you much good at the lower court level, but it could well protect your interests if and when you appeal.

The party who files an appeal has already completed some process where a ruling has been issued that is not, in that party's opinion, entirely satisfactory. The next group of judges who looks at that case is going to assume that the original court had the best opportunity to review all the facts of the case. As I learned in my suit with the Sowerwine family, it is difficult to get an appellate court to overturn a lower court's decision. There must be some compelling reason; the lower court overlooked relevant precedent, statute or rule of court, or the lower court overlooked or misconstrued one or more material facts of record. The primary objective of the appellate court is to make certain that the law was applied properly – they will review the facts, but often in a cursory fashion. The courts are overburdened and often are unable to give each case the consideration it deserves. It is therefore incumbent upon the appellant (the individual filing the appeal) to provide the court with a clear, concise statement of the reason for the appeal. The court's attention must be brought to focus on the salient issues, with all else pushed aside.

By way of example, in the State of Pennsylvania, the Supreme Court mandates:

"The failure of a petitioner to present with accuracy, brevity and clearness whatever is essential to a ready and adequate understanding of the points requiring consideration will be a sufficient reason for denying the petition (for appeal)."

That rule of court couldn't be any more straightforward. The judges will not spend time sifting through piles of documents or reading voluminous dissertations in order to determine whether or not there are grounds for appeal. It is up to the appellant to present the court with a convincing summation that is clear and concise, or the appeal will be denied – regardless of the merit of the appeal. Once you understand this, you will also understand that the judges are not going to reread entire transcripts of a trial, nor are they going to analyze all of the documents that were offered up as evidence in the trial. They will assume that a capable and competent judge has already done that at the lower court level. They will not retry the case; that's not the purpose of an appellate court. The scope of the appeal will be very narrow, and the judges will focus on the misinterpretation or misapplication of law and grievous procedural errors. Period.

The appeal process varies from state to state, but in general a first appeal is automatically granted. A second is not. This means that the appeal brief filed with an appellate court must be a compelling document. Your attorney may have as little as 5 to 15 minutes to make your case in front of the court, so the document itself must be convincing. Your attorney's remarks must be on point and brief. The court must not be allowed to sense any uncertainty in the appeal brief or in the oral presentation.

This is an appropriate place to mention a procedural option that is available to you in most courts as you wend your way through a series of hearings. Most courts allow you to hire a court reporter to create a transcript of the discussion that goes on at a hearing. For some hearings, this may not be appropriate (pre-trial hearing, perhaps). However, whenever you feel that it might be beneficial to have an accurate record of what is said in the courtroom, and by whom, petition the court to allow you to provide a court reporter. Some courts actually have the ability to provide you with a videotape of the proceedings. In either case, you will have to pay for the tape or the transcript, but it will be money well spent.

I find the written transcript easier to refer to than a videotape, but the tape does allow you to view a person's demeanor and listen to the inflection of their voice when they speak at court. That could have value in certain circumstances. I highly recommend using the services of a court reporter anytime there is an opportunity to do so. I will guarantee you that should you appeal, the court record will become a significant source of information for you during your preparation.

The process leading up to the appeal is less intense than the process that precedes the initial trial. Once you've prepared for trial, you should have collected and organized the information in such a way that the appeal brief becomes a cut-and-paste job to a great extent, unless some new factual evidence has surfaced since you received the lower court's decision.

That's both a good thing and a bad thing. During the time you are awaiting your appeal – a period of time that might exceed a year – it is easy to forget those significant little things that were so poignant during trial preparation. It becomes the individual's responsibility to stay "tuned in" to the case and to make sure counsel does the same. Remember that your attorney has many other clients with cases that are as important to them as your case is to you. Your attorney is involved with them just as he/she is with you. It therefore becomes much easier for you to keep your focus concerning your case over a protracted period of time than it is for your attorney to maintain the same degree of familiarity with the facts. Even during the quiet times, when there is nothing to file and nothing to do but wait for your appeal hearing, keep a dialogue going with your attorney. It will cost you money – every hour is billable – but in the long run I think you will find it a prudent use of your resources. Don't be a pest, but drop a note to your lawyer or give a call when you have a pertinent thought. Keep your mind working on the case and periodically engage your attorney's mind as well. It will be much easier for your counsel to step back into your case at the appropriate time if he/she was never really allowed to step out of it entirely.

Again, a first appeal is generally guaranteed; a second appeal is not. If you lose on your initial appeal, you will probably have the option of appealing to a higher court – perhaps the state Supreme Court. However, that court will not be obligated to hear your appeal. For Supreme Court judges to grant an appeal there must be something about the lower courts' decisions that appear so egregious they feel compelled to intervene. Courts become busier each year, and the ability to be heard at the Supreme Court level becomes much more difficult. There are too many requests for appeal and not enough time to hear them all. By necessity, the courts must be very discriminatory with regard to the number and type of cases they choose to hear.

If you do appeal to a higher court and your appeal is granted, the process will seem very familiar. You will file your brief, wait for your hearing to be scheduled, your counsel will have a few minutes to present oral arguments before the court on your behalf, and you will wait for months for the decision.

Here is another word of wisdom from the voice of experience:

If you go through this entire process from start to finish, convinced that you are right and that you will be vindicated by the court, and if that doesn't happen – you lose – don't allow that experience to ruin your life. You won't feel very cheery, but the best advise is the lyrical offering served up by Frank Sinatra many years ago:

"Pick yourself up, dust yourself off, start all over again."

When I lost the case to Sowerwine in the 1980s I was devastated. I lost the case, I lost all our money, and I lost my personal pride. Believe me, when you lose at court you feel that everyone assumes you were in the wrong all along. You are certain everyone is saying:

He talked a good game, but there must have been something he wasn't telling us because the court found against him – and we all know the courts are right and just.

If that's not really how people view you after you lose, it doesn't matter. That's how it feels.

It will take time for your wounds to heal, but the amazing thing is that they will heal. It's not easy picking up the pieces and starting over, especially if this happens to you later in life. You may not feel like you have the energy to begin again, but the human psyche is an incredible apparatus. You will find the energy and the resolve to begin again, precisely because you won't like where you are in your life. You will be able to pull your life back together, to recreate wealth, to regain your self-esteem and to become a whole person again. Yes, it will take time and it will take effort, but you can do it. The alternative is to become an angry person, consumed by self-pity – and that's not an option, in my estimation.

Win or lose, at the point when it's no longer painful to reflect on your courtroom experience, take the time to ponder what you have been through. Think about what you did right and what you could have done better. Consider how your opposition handled their side of the case and try to understand how their actions helped or harmed them. I realize the frustration this exercise can cause, but if you ever find yourself back in court – Heaven forbid! – what you learn from this experience could be of immense benefit.

I learned a great deal from my first introduction to the legal process in 1982. Once I could think about it rationally, I realized that I, and my counsel, had made some tactical mistakes. Some could have been avoided and some, perhaps, could not. I have tried to learn from my experiences at court and I think my analysis has served me well. While I did not prevail in later litigation against LSI, I do believe that my counsel and I made every effort to do all that we could in order to win. We fought a good fight against very difficult odds, given the financial and political resources of my opponent.

I will add that in writing this text, I have learned as well. This endeavor has forced me to pull out court documents, some of which I haven't read for years. It has been surprising to me how the passage of time can skew one's memory of events. It took a good deal of reading and investigation to put things back into perspective so I could give a factual account of my experiences. This exercise, performed years after my first courtroom experience, has helped me to see what I might have done differently to insure a better outcome.

Just as I have learned from this experience, I hope that by reading about my trials (literally) and tribulations you have developed a better understanding of our legal system. The complexities are limitless, but what I have recounted for you here should provide basic knowledge that you can expand and tailor to your individual needs, should the occasion arise.

CONCLUSION

It is my belief that most Americans who become intimately involved with our legal system have an imperfect idea of how the system works. It's not like Court TV, especially when you and your loved ones are the main characters. It's not a perfect system; it's a difficult process, it's not always fair, and it requires your full commitment. Since my first introduction to our system and my earliest disappointments, I have given a great deal of thought to how our system of jurisprudence might be improved. I have come to the conclusion that the system has been engineered properly; it's the human factor that creates the problems with the judicial process, just as it is with many other things in life. If all people were honest, honorable and intelligent, we would have less need for our court system, and it in turn would function in a more just and appropriate fashion. People are the problem – not the system.

I will add a couple of caveats to my conclusion. There is one problem with the system that is an outgrowth of a people problem. A litigant's victory at court and an attorney's professional status are both measured by winning a favorable verdict – usually accompanied by a reasonable monetary award. Winning, therefore, has become the all-important end. The means to that end have become very secondary. In my opinion, this results-oriented process encourages litigants to lie, witnesses to prostitute themselves, and attorneys to endorse and participate in these practices. The goal is not to root out evil or promote justice. The goal is to win – at all costs. Law firms that have a record of winning a high percentage of the time prosper and become socially and politically significant. They can become so powerful that they can influence judicial appointments and/or elections. This can, and does, result in a corruption of the system. This is perhaps a people problem, but it is the design of the system that encourages the abuse. However, to reform the system to correct this deficiency, an entirely new benchmark for "winning" would have to be established. Unfortunately, there is no better yardstick than the number of favorable decisions earned and the amount of awards received. The flaw is easily identified; the fix is deceptive.

A second problem is one that I alluded to in the section entitled *Misconception: Judges are Infallible.* It has been eloquently revealed in John Grisham's book entitled *The Appeal*, published in 2008. The story deals with the manner in which judges are selected and is a frightening, but true-to-life, tale about justice deprived (or perhaps denied) by the direct influence of big business on the court system.

In the book, a man who deals in the business of managing judicial elections for special interests displays a map with all fifty states colored either green or yellow. He says:

"Thirty-one states elect their appellate and supreme court judges. They are in green. The yellow ones have the good sense to appoint their courts. We make our living in the green ones."

The unfortunate truth is that special interests can and do influence judges, and thereby influence their decisions. More often than we'd like to acknowledge, judges ignore legal and factual information presented at court in order to render opinions that conform to particular political or philosophical leanings. It is unfortunate, yet important, to realize that judges often gain and retain their seats for that very reason.

Mr. Grisham sums up the problem quite nicely, saying:

"As long as private money is allowed in judicial elections we will see competing interests fight for seats on the bench."

He implies, by way of comment and by reference to his story, that the results can be detrimental to the health of our judicial system.

For years, there have been attempts to reform the civil justice system, and a number of state and federal laws have been (and continue to be) passed to that end. Most of these laws have limited the circumstances under which injured people can sue, and/or limited the amount of damages a jury can award injured parties. These reforms are important – they reduce the number and severity of nuisance suits filed against individuals and companies by people who have been recruited by unscrupulous lawyers in search of a slice of damage awards. To these lawyers, the severity of the damage – even the reality of the damage – is unimportant. The game is played to achieve quick settlements from decent citizens or honest business people who want to avoid the cost and uncertain outcome of litigation. While these reforms don't address the underlying issue of fairness that is eroded by the concept that winning overrides the need to flesh out justice, they are nonetheless significant.

There is one additional problem with our legal system that is frequently overlooked – often not even recognized as a problem. It is also one of the easiest flaws to correct. The problem is individual reluctance to accept jury duty. Most of us recognize that one of our responsibilities as U.S. citizens is to serve as jurors if called upon. However, there is perhaps no service that is more shunned and no duty that people try harder to avoid. The reason is not necessarily that the duty itself is repugnant; the reason is that jury duty is never convenient.

I confess that I have been guilty of trying to avoid jury duty. I was called once when I lived in Colorado and decided long before I reported for duty that I was going to find a way to get out of it. As it turned out, I didn't have to try to get excused – I wasn't selected.

The case involved a young man who had shot and wounded an acquaintance following a dispute of some sort that took place at a late-night party. Witnesses had seen the shooting and reported that both the shooter and the victim had been drinking heavily and taking drugs. The shooter had one prior felony conviction involving a firearm, and he had served several years in prison for the offense. During jury selection the defense attorney asked me if my judgment in the case would be influenced by the knowledge that the defendant was a convicted felon. I said it certainly would, and I asked him why drug charges hadn't been filed in addition to the count of attempted murder. He told me I could go.

I gave an honest answer and I was excused. That was appropriate; I would not have been an open-minded juror. To this day it is difficult for me to comprehend that there were twelve people who responded to the defense counsel's question in a way that convinced him they could be impartial. But that's not the point. The point is that I walked into that courtroom with the intent of avoiding jury duty. That was *in*appropriate.

There is a significant portion of the population who cannot get a fair trial by a jury of their peers because their peers find a way to avoid jury duty. We should all readjust our thinking when it comes to this social obligation. What might seem a ridiculous waste of time to us could be the most important event in someone else's life.

The answer to this problem, then, is simple. We should all be accepting of our responsibility and serve as best we can when called for jury duty. I will add, however, that many jurisdictions could encourage us to take our obligation more seriously if they would be more sensitive to the fact that it is an imposition and at best inconvenient. For some, taking time off from life to serve as a juror is more difficult than others. Perhaps courts could do a better job of acknowledging this, and try to refine their scheduling process accordingly. In New Mexico, for example, a person who is empanelled for jury duty is on-call for 90 days. During those three months, they can be required to show up at the courthouse on any given day and assigned to a trial of any duration. Life gets put on hold for three full months. I think that is too much to expect of young mothers with children at home, business owners who have companies to run, people who are caregivers to the elderly, and many others whose circumstances do not allow them to take a 90-day hiatus from life.

Despite its shortcomings, I would encourage anyone who has been wronged to consider the recourse available within our legal system. Don't be quick to bring suit against another – especially if there is any possibility of working things out without going to court. However, if matters cannot be settled, don't run away from a lawsuit if you believe you are truly on solid ground both factually and legally, and have the financial and emotional resources to fight the fight.

I would like to offer one last piece of advice. If and when you enter into an agreement with another party, pay close attention to the provisions of your agreement and avoid, if possible, ambiguous clauses that might lead to misinterpretation or misunderstanding down the road. Don't try to "slip one by" contractually, and don't fall victim to that tactic yourself. Face all the pertinent issues up-front and head-on. And above all – and this is *really* important – above all, don't enter into any agreement or relationship with someone you believe to be of poor character. This is the greatest lesson I have learned during my more than 40 years in business.

I acknowledge that it's not always easy to assess the character of a person or an entity with whom you choose to do business. When I purchased the ranch from E. O. Sowerwine, Jr. in 1981, I knew I was dealing with someone whose character I questioned. He was, at the very least, eccentric. Although he was an intelligent man, Sowerwine was a self-professed libertarian who objected to paying taxes (and who told me he didn't) and who – when the going got tough – even denied he was a U.S. citizen subject to the laws of the land. Instead, he claimed Nicaraguan citizenship, related to his years of work in that country. He was notorious for ignoring his monetary obligations, and at the time he came to me for help, the mortgage on his property had been in default for a very long time. Regardless of the merits of the purchase and the comprehensiveness of the contract, I should have avoided the deal. You just don't do business with those you don't trust.

When I sold the Software to LSI in 1997, I had no such qualms. After all, I was dealing directly with the legal staff of Merrill Lynch, and Merrill Lynch owned LSI in its entirety. What reason would I have to suspect the integrity of one of the world's financial giants? Big surprise!

What I have since learned from discussions with entrepreneurs and independent businessmen who have had similar experiences dealing with large national and multi-national companies is this:

Some business schools and many business mentors teach and preach the creed I call "Promise them anything." When engaging in a contract, they are willing to make promises they have no intention of fulfilling, just for the sake of making the deal. They know they can and will have the opportunity to address matters they facetiously agreed to when they arise at some later date. When they do – when they are confronted with non-performance – they have options. They can perform, if they so choose. If they elect not to perform, they can try to renegotiate the obtrusive issue or they can ignore it. If they ignore it, in essence inviting the other party to sue, they can see where that road leads them. It might result in a settlement that reduces their cost or the extent of their obligations. If a claimant, unwilling to settle, presses suit, he or she might fail to survive the legal battle of attrition and fall by the wayside. If the matter happens to make it to court, the chances are good that the claimant can be defeated by a slick, well-connected cadre of lawyers. In fact, the only real risk is that the claimant will win at court and be awarded damages that exceed what it would have cost to perform as originally agreed.

Bottom line: If you renege on a promise, odds are that you'll be able to terminate the matter for less than the original promise would have cost you anyway. Promise them anything. Deal with it later.

That, in my opinion, was LSI's philosophy from the onset of the purchase of our valuation Software. Their actions (or inactions) make it difficult to interpret their intentions any other way. More appalling is the fact that LSI's parent companies – first Merrill Lynch and later Fidelity National

Financial – must have been aware of LSI's intentions. If they weren't, shame on them for not paying closer attention to a wholly owned subsidiary – especially one that racked up attorney fees and costs attributable to this litigation in excess of $360,000 by the end of 2006 (according to court documents). Who knows how monumental that cost became by the time the litigation ended two years later? On the other hand, if they *were* aware of LSI's intentions, shame on them for condoning such business practices.

My understanding about these types of business practices was reinforced when I was in Pittsburgh for our hearing in front of the Superior Court of Pennsylvania on March 18, 2008. The evening before the hearing I was having dinner at a restaurant a few blocks from the District Courthouse, sitting at the bar because I didn't want to take table space for just myself during a busy hour. A gentleman sat down beside me and after few moments we struck up a conversation. He asked where I was from and why I was in town, and I told him. He asked several questions that led me to believe he was more knowledgeable about court matters than most. I asked if he was a lawyer, and he said he was. Not only was he a lawyer, but he taught law classes at a local university. After a lengthy discussion he asked,

"Why didn't you just ignore your agreements with LSI and let <u>them</u> sue <u>you</u>? You could have kept or swiped a copy of the Software, and if you never became a commercial threat to them, they would have probably ignored your actions. You would have what you bargained for and you wouldn't be here today fighting to get to court."

I replied that I had put my name on agreements. I had given my word, and I was honor-bound to comply with the terms of those agreements. He said that was nice sentiment but stupid business practice. LSI's attorneys had previously implied in similar fashion that we should have ignored LSI's failures to act and taken matters into our own hands. We had access to the Software at LSI; we should have taken it if they wouldn't deliver a copy as they were obligated to do. Likewise, knowing that LSI was obligated to release us from our non-compete agreement, we should have ignored the agreement whether they delivered the release or not. The implication was clear – we were somehow remiss for complying with the contracts. It shouldn't have been LSI's concern.

I was appalled at the man's suggestion that we should have disregarded our written agreements, and I told the man as much. He just shrugged his shoulders. He observed correctly that I was now forced to sue LSI to protect my rights under our agreements and that I would have, in all probability, been better off breaching the contracts myself and letting LSI sue me. He said that's how business is done. I asked him how a commercial environment can remain viable if no one honors their commitments, and he commented it all has a way of working out. I thought to myself, "and he's teaching our next generation of lawyers!"

Am I naïve to believe that contracts are made to be honored rather than broken? What I am hearing from professors of law and business is that I am out of touch with reality and have little chance of surviving in the world of commerce. I disagree. If most business people were not honorable, our system of commerce would collapse.

Theodore Roosevelt seems to have shared my views (or I, his). In *An Autobiography*, published in 1913, he states:

But, doubtless chiefly through my own fault, some of the teaching of the law books and of the classroom seemed to me to be against justice. The caveat emptor side of the law, like the caveat emptor side of business, seemed to me repellent; it did not make for social fair dealing. The "let the buyer beware" maxim, when translated into actual practice, whether in law or business, tends to translate itself further into the seller making his profit at the expense of the buyer, instead of by a bargain which shall be to the profit of both. It did not seem to me that the law was framed to discourage as it should sharp practice, and all other kinds of bargains except those which are fair and of benefit to both sides.

I must confess that I initially had a gut feeling that LSI would be a dishonorable partner. When I looked back over our years of correspondence in preparation for our lawsuit, I found that we wrote them regarding their failure to perform before we even consummated the final Purchase Agreement on September 30, 1997. In the months prior to closing, LSI had failed, among other things, to adhere to the agreed-upon timetable for the delivery of draft agreements, and they had made disturbing comments about the commitments they had made and were about to make. We began to believe they were being insincere about their interest in the Software. By September 11th the situation had become so frustrating that my partner wrote to LSI saying:

"Need I remind you that it was ____ (attorney for Merrill Lynch) who said that the Letter of Intent (from LSI to ESI) was meaningless and that all our prior agreements meant nothing. I don't get a "warm and fuzzy feeling" of trust from that."

I guess we should have seen what was coming. I felt the sale and resulting relationship made such perfect sense that my ability to make a prudent decision was clouded. My mistake. I'll try to be more disciplined next time, and trust my intuition.

And regardless of my experiences, there *will* be a next time. I won't stop doing business because some of my transactions have resulted in litigation, nor will I cease my endeavors because I've had unfortunate experiences at court. I won't shrink from opportunity for fear that someone will once again try to cheat me. That would be the ultimate defeat. I won't do that, and don't you do that either.

AFTERWORD

Stockton et al vs. Velasquez, and subsequently Rio Arriba County, NM vs. Stockton et al (2003)

In December of 2007, Rio Arriba County filed an appeal with the New Mexico Appellate Court. In their brief, filed January 2, 2008, they reiterated all their same old arguments. No new factual information was included. The County simply disagreed with Judge Hall's decision and asked that it be overturned because Judge Hall had arrived at the wrong conclusion.

Some of the Rio Arriba County Commissioners, as well as the County Manager, have stated that they will move to condemn our private road for public use if they are unsuccessful in their appeal. Since the road goes only to private homes and does not access public lands, the County will presumably have to condemn some area for public use in addition to the road. I think they underestimate the task before them; perhaps I underestimate them. Time will tell.

I considered delaying the publication of this book until this case was resolved. If it does end up in an action for condemnation, I'm sure I will learn some important tidbits to pass along to readers. However, in the midst of the appeal and in an effort to avoid condemnation, we are bogged down in mediation – and have been for many months. If I wait for a resolution, it could be years before I go to press. I have consequently decided to go forward with this book; perhaps there will be a second edition that includes the as-yet-unresolved ending to this litigation. Stay tuned.

Evaluation Services, Inc. vs. Lender's Service, Inc. (2004)

In January of 2008, after the Superior Court of Pennsylvania refused to reconsider their decision in our case against LSI, we filed an appeal with the Pennsylvania Supreme Court. On October 3rd, we received their answer:

***"AND NOW**, this 1st day of October, 2008, the Petition for Allowance of Appeal is **DENIED**."*

After four years, hundreds of hours of preparation and tens of thousands of dollars, we were denied our day in court in no uncertain terms, in a single sentence. We would not have our day in court on this issue in the State of Pennsylvania.

Evaluation Services, Inc. vs. Lender's Service, Inc. (2006)

The hearing on our appeal before the Superior Court of Pennsylvania was held on March 18, 2008. Prior to the hearing, my attorney prepared and filed a masterful brief that pinpointed the errors made by the Court of Common Pleas and gave good and ample reason why the Superior Court should overturn Judge Judith Friedman's decision. At hearing it became very apparent from the questions asked that the judges on the Superior Court had failed to read our brief. Nonetheless, my counsel put forth a concise yet forceful argument in favor of our position.

On June 6, 2008, the Superior Court issued its opinion, ruling against us and upholding Judge Friedman's decision. The Opinion, a formal Opinion written by Judge Bender (which will likely be published for precedential citation) states:

"Having determined that ESI waived its right to arbitrate, and that the claim for breach of the implied covenant of good faith and fair dealing is subsumed in a breach of contract

claim, we conclude that the trial court correctly granted LSI's motion for judgment on the pleadings and denied ESI's cross-motion to direct arbitration."

In plain language, this means that according to the Pennsylvania Superior Court from this day forward a claim for a breach of the implied covenant of good faith and fair dealing will be deemed to be included within a breach of contract claim. This effectively converts all claims for breach of the implied covenant of good faith and fair dealing into breach of contract claims. By so ruling, the Superior Court of Pennsylvania has determined that a breach of contract is a breach of contract regardless of whether the breach was committed intentionally (in bad faith) or inadvertently. I contend the two are vastly different and the seriousness of the one (a bad faith dealing) should be viewed much more severely than the other (an accidental breach). Regardless, the courts in Pennsylvania will hereafter consider the one (breach of good faith) to be the other (breach of contract), unless and until the Superior Court's ruling is overturned.

We filed an appeal with the Pennsylvania Supreme Court, not simply because the Opinion handed down by the Superior Court was obtuse, but because it made no sense in the context of our particular case. Our original agreements with LSI anticipated the possibility of bad-faith conduct, defined in the Software Purchase Agreement as "willful misconduct or intentional non-performance." The bargain between the parties expressly required good faith in the transaction and the relationship. Therefore, it was inappropriate to conclude that a breach of the covenant of good faith claim was nothing more than a breach of contract claim.

The Pennsylvania Supreme Court disagreed. On November 17th, 2008, we received word that our appeal had been denied. Strike two; we're out.

One Other Noteworthy Item

On June 25, 2008, our would-be trial judge—Judge Eugene Scanlon—announced that he would resign the bench effective July 7th. Judge Scanlon had been appointed to the court in 1998 by the Governor, and was elected to a 10 year term in 1999. He worked in the family division of the Allegheny County Pennsylvania Court of Common Pleas prior to being elevated to the civil division in 2005. He brought with him a reputation as a fair arbiter in the messiest of disputes between relations – high praise for a most difficult assignment.

It was stated in his announcement that he was resigning to work in "private mediation and alternative dispute resolution." It is unusual for a judge to leave the security of the Court of Common Pleas for private business with its attendant risks. I would like to think that Judge Scanlon decided he didn't have the stomach for the politics associated with his job on the bench. I'll never know.

AND SO …

All but one of our legal battles are behind us now. Despite being weary of litigation, my neighbors, my wife and I continue with our remaining fight against Uvaldo Velasquez and Rio Arriba County because it is, in our opinions, a fight to be fought. We believe in the integrity of our position and refuse to allow others to take unfair advantage of us simply because they believe their greater resources permit them to do so.

There is no doubt that the legal system in the United States favors those who have the most resources with which to do battle, but a wealth of resources does not necessarily guarantee success. Sometimes an opponent with perseverance and a strong belief in a cause can be an ominous foe. After all these years and many disappointments, I may be naïve, but I still believe justice will prevail.

Having arrived at the end of this narrative – an account of court battles where I obviously believe I held the high moral ground, yet lost in nearly every instance – I sense the reader might be asking, "Is this guy misrepresenting his experiences or is he just stupid?' It's that "stigma thing" again. All I can say is that my representation of the cases has been honest and complete. I haven't withheld facts that might have reflected poorly on my positions, nor have I embellished the inappropriate actions of others. That logically leads to the conclusion that I am just stupid.

I can't offer much in defense of my intellect except to say the fights I have fought were, in my opinion, battles worth fighting. I have believed strongly in my positions and have believed just as strongly that others were trying to take advantage of me. I believed I could and would win. That might be viewed as dimwitted given the outcomes, but the outcomes were not apparent when I entered the fights.

Had I lived in another era, these fights might have been resolved by a duel at twenty paces or a gunfight on a dusty, deserted street at high noon. Given my success ratio, I would have expired or been severely wounded after my first fight. Today, our society offers a much more civilized approach – instead of a gun, someone sticks an attorney in your back and demands all your money. While the outcome can be devastating, at least you can live to fight again.

And so, I live to fight again. I sincerely hope my battles are behind me. I don't enjoy these "adventures" and am not litigious by nature. But if you were to ask whether I would do it all over again, given the exact same circumstances, I'd have to answer, "Yes, I would."

Just stupid, I guess.

MY ADVICE TO YOU

Throughout this book I have offered my thoughts and advice regarding many facets of the litigation process. I have compiled a single list of those items in bullet-point format below, each referencing the page in the book where the discussion leading up to the advice can be found.

Beginning at:

GLOSSARY

All definitions have been taken from Wikipedia as of 12/20/2008.

Appeal

In an appeal on the record from a decision in a judicial proceeding, both appellant and respondent are bound to base their arguments wholly on the proceedings and body of evidence as they were presented in the lower tribunal. Each seeks to prove to the higher court that the result they desired was the just result. Precedent and case law figure prominently in the arguments. In order for the appeal to succeed, the appellant must prove that the lower court committed reversible error, that is, an impermissible action by the court acted to cause a result that was unjust, and which would not have resulted had the court acted properly.

Breach

Breach of contract is a legal concept in which a binding agreement or bargained-for exchange is not honored by one or more of the parties to the contract by non-performance or interference with the other party's performance. A *material breach* is any failure to perform that permits the other party to the contract to either compel performance, or collect damages because of the breach

Civil Law

In the common law, civil law refers to the area of laws, which through incorporation, take on the legal status of individuals. Civil law, in this sense, is usually referred to in comparison to criminal law, which is that body of law involving the state against individuals (including incorporated organizations) where the state relies on the power given it by statutory law.

The objective of civil law is different to other types of law. In civil law there is the attempt to right a wrong, honor an agreement, or settle a dispute. If there is a victim, they get compensation, and the person who is the cause of the wrong pays, this being a civilized form of, or legal alternative to, revenge.

Claim

A claim is a legal action to obtain money, property or the enforcement of a right protected by law against another party

Complaint

A Complaint is a formal legal document that sets out the basic facts and legal reasons (causes of action) that the filing party (the plaintiffs) believes are sufficient to support a claim against another person, persons, entity or entities (the defendants) that entitles the plaintiff(s) to a remedy (either money damages or injunctive relief).

Court of Common Pleas

In United States jurisprudence, Court of Common Pleas is a court of certain jurisdiction. It stems from the Court of Common Pleas in the English legal system and was brought to the United States by the colonial settlers along with the rest of the English common law tradition. In the United States legal system, there are at least four states which currently have Courts of Common Pleas, among them, Pennsylvania.

Defendant

A defendant or defender is any party who is required to answer the complaint of a plaintiff or pursuer in a civil lawsuit before a court,

Deposition

In law, a deposition is evidence given under oath and recorded for use in court at a later date. In many countries depositions are given in courtrooms, but in the United States they are given outside a courtroom in certain well-defined circumstances. In the U.S. it is a part of the discovery process in which litigants obtain information from each other in preparation for trial.

Estoppel

Estoppel is a legal doctrine recognized both at common law and in equity in various forms. It is meant to complement the requirement of consideration in contract law. In general it protects a party who would suffer detriment if:

- The defendant has done or said something to induce an expectation
- The plaintiff relied (reasonably) on the expectation and would suffer detriment if that expectation were false.

Governing Law

The body of law of a particular jurisdiction which governs the rights and responsibilities of parties in a given situation.

Jurisdiction

Jurisdiction is the authority given to a legal body, or to a political leader (Prime Minister, President, etc.) to deal with legal matters, and to pronounce or enforce legal matters.

Jurisprudence

Jurisprudence is the theory and philosophy of law.

Jury Trial

The right to trial by jury is guaranteed by the 7th Amendment, which provides: "In Suits at common law, where the value in controversy shall exceed twenty dollars, the right of trial by jury shall be preserved, and no fact tried by a jury shall be otherwise re-examined in any Court of the United States, than according to the rules of the common law."

The right to a jury trial in civil cases does not extend to the states, however, except when a state court is enforcing a federally created right, of which the right to trial by jury is a substantial part. Following the English tradition, U.S. juries have usually been composed of 12 jurors, and the jury's verdict has usually been required to be unanimous. However, in many jurisdictions, the number of jurors is often reduced to a lesser number (such as five or six) by legislative enactment, or by agreement of both sides. Some jurisdictions also permit a verdict to be returned despite the dissent of one, two, or three jurors.

Litigant

A party involved in a lawsuit. A litigant is a person suing or being sued, or otherwise calling upon the judicial process to determine the outcome of a suit. This does not include witnesses or other persons who may be called to court during a trial - just the parties themselves.

Litigate

In American law, a lawsuit is a civil action brought before a court in which the party commencing the action, the plaintiff, seeks a legal remedy. One or more defendants are required to respond to the plaintiff's complaint. If the plaintiff is successful, judgment will be given in the plaintiff's favor, and a range of court orders may be issued to enforce a right, award damages, or impose an injunction to prevent an act or compel an act. The conduct of a lawsuit is called litigation.

Perjury

Perjury is the act of lying or making verifiably false statements on a material matter under oath or affirmation in a court of law or in any of various sworn statements in writing. Perjury is a crime because the witness has sworn to tell the truth and, for the credibility of the court, witness testimony must be relied on as being truthful.

Plaintiff

A plaintiff, also known as a claimant or complainant, is the party who initiates a lawsuit (also known as an *action*) before a court. By doing so, the plaintiff seeks a legal remedy, and if successful, the court will issue judgment in favor of the plaintiff and make the appropriate court order (eg. an order for damages).

Quiet Title Action

An action to quiet title is a lawsuit brought in a court having jurisdiction over land disputes, in order to establish a party's title to real property against anyone and everyone, and thus "quiet" any challenges or claims to the title.

Restraining Order

A restraining order is a legal order issued by a state court which requires one person to stop harming another person. While there are differences from state to state, all protective order statutes permit the court to order the abuser to stay away from someone, their home, their workplace or their school ("stay away" provisions) and to stop contacting them.

Superior Court

In Pennsylvania, the Superior Court is an appellate court.

Supreme Court

Each U.S. state has a state supreme court, though some do not actually use the term "supreme court." The Supreme Court of Pennsylvania is the court of last resort for the Commonwealth of Pennsylvania.

Tort

Tort is the law of civil wrongs. Tort law usually provides people with the rights to compensation when another person harms their legally protected interests.

Venue

Venue deals with locality of a lawsuit, that is, with questions of which court or courts with proper jurisdiction may hear a specific suit.